Williams Outing Club

North Berkshire Outdoor Guide

Text by members of the
Williams Outing Club

Edited by Willard S. Morgan '96

Map by Ethan B. Plunkett '00
and Patrick D. Dunlavey

WILLIAMSTOWN, MASSACHUSETTS

Please note: The Williams Outing Club assumes no responsibility for the safety of any users of this guide. It is understood that travel in the North Berkshire area involves certain risks and that the readers of this guide are liable for their own actions. Please read the Preparation sections carefully and expect the unexpected.

Williams Outing Club
North Berkshire Outdoor Guide
North Berkshire Trails

© 1999 by the President and Trustees of Williams College
No portion of this book may be reproduced in any form without permission from the publisher.

Book Design by Willard S. Morgan '96
Cover Design and artwork by Hilary D. Williams '01

Published by the Williams Outing Club
1004 Baxter Hall
Williams College
Williamstown, MA 01267

For ordering information contact the Williams Outing Club at the above address or by phone at (413)597-2317
Printed by Excelsior Printing
North Adams, MA

Printed on recycled paper with soy-based ink.

Revised and updated 9th edition of the WOC Trail Guide

ISBN 0-9669785-0-1

Second printing July, 2002

10 9 8 7 6 5 4 3 2

TABLE OF CONTENTS

Maps, Photos and Illustrations

ODE TO THE GUIDE

Sons of the towns and cities,
Where'er your home abode,
Come straight unto my doorway
By steam or Trolley Road,
Glide swift on automobiles,
Walk up, or easier ride,
And you will better know me –
If you bring along this Guide.

Come not with rod or level,
With compass and with chain,
To measure heights and bases,
But coats to shed the rain;
Leave cameras behind you
My peaks and scars snap,
For you will best enjoy me
This Guide Book in your lap.

You may sleep upon my summit
With your head upon my breast,
The companion of my silence,
A partaker of my rest,
You may come with all your fixings,
And behold my every side,
But you'll never really know me
Unless you have this Guide.

From the *Pathfinder to Greylock Mountain*
The Berkshire Hills and Historic Bennington
By Col. W.H. Philips 1910

ACKNOWLEDGEMENTS

D ozens of people have contributed to the completion of the *North Berkshire Outdoor Guide*, a book truly written by committee. The Williams Outing Club (WOC) and Williams College are not for profit and much of the time devoted to this project was volunteered for the good of the college and local community.

First, a thanks to all the Williams students of years past who published the first eight editions of the *WOC Trail Guide*, starting with *The Mountains of Eph* in 1927. The eighth edition, edited by Jim Lerczak '88 and printed in 1988, provided the springboard for this ninth edition.

The WOC Executive Boards from 1994 to 1999 have contributed extensively through brainstormed ideas, field checking and reading of draft material. Many other Williams students, WOC members or not, volunteered their time as well.

In a never-ending quest for answers to obscure questions regarding the North Berkshire area, a number of individuals stand out for offering their knowledge. Bob Hatton knows every twist and turn of trail in the Mt. Greylock State Reservation and he was quick to give help and advice. Paul Karabinos has combed the region for rock outcrops and accumulated a vast trove of information for exploring on or off trails in the North Berkshire area. Hank Art was always available to answer questions regarding natural history, environmental issues or Hopkins Memorial Forest. Leslie Reed-Evans provided information on the Taconic Range, local trail initiatives and the Williamstown Rural Lands Foundation. Lauren Stevens shared his experience writing Berkshire County hiking and skiing guides to help start our project and offered helpful advice throughout the entire process.

Several people contributed writing for the new sections covering trip preparation and other outdoor activities. Thanks to Dan Bolnick '96, Cordelia Dickinson '98, Noah Federman '97, Monica Goracke '97, Ethan Gutmann '99, Darby Jack '97, Megan Lawson '98, Deb Zucker '97, and Scott Lewis.

Others have offered their constructive feedback on a series of drafts. We appreciate the efforts of Juliane Austin '99, Brendan Burns '98, Dan Center '01, Chris Elkington '98, Erryn Leinbaugh '99, Ethan Plunkett '99, Becky Sanborn '01, Jack Drury, Pat Dunlavey, Rene Laubach, Hank Art, Kai Lee, Scott Lewis, Leslie Reed-Evans, Lauren Stevens and Peter Wells.

Those who checked trail descriptions include: A.J. Bernheim '96, Antony Blaikie '99, Dan Bolnick '96, Kate Boyle '97, Jeremy Burr '99, Alison Davies '99, Nathan Day '97, Chris Elkington '98, Sylvia Englund '99, Jeff Gould '98, Tim Gustafson '98, Mike Heep '99, Steve Hufnagel '96, Darby Jack '97, Glen Kelly '97, Megan Lawson '98, Josh Lawton '97, Jen Newton '99, Liz Rumsey '96, Jay Schuur '96, Juliette Spertus '97, Joel Tolman '98, Chuck Wall '97, and Cosmo Catalano.

A project of this size drew help from many others in big and small ways. Amrita Ahuja '98, Taylor Schildgen '00, Aya Reiss '00, Jim Heyes '96, Emily King '99, Kyle Nagle '96, Laura Smith '99, Kristine Taylor '01, Seth Battis '98, Jen Newton '98, Hilary Williams '01, Heather Clemow, Liliane DeCock, Art Evans, Marcus Johnson, Douglas Morgan and Catherine Wolfe all helped to make this guide a reality.

Special thanks to Cordelia Dickinson '98, who shouldered the burden of moving this guide toward publication in 1997 and 1998. Corey effectively compiled all the draft material into a manuscript and solicited reader feedback. Her careful research provided numerous historical notes you will find scattered throughout this book.

A project unto itself, the *North Berkshire Trails* map demanded the devotion of a committed cadre of students. Nathan Foster '98, Darby Jack '97, Willard Morgan '96, Katherine Birnie '00, Cordelia Dickinson '98, and Emily Piendak '99, started the process. However, Ethan Plunkett '99 adopted the project as his own, painstakingly digitized information from USGS maps and surveyed trails in the field. The greatest of thanks to Pat Dunlavey who refined the map data into a final form with his extensive professional cartographic experience.

Scott Lewis (WOC Director) has kept this project alive through a revolving Williams student body over five years. He devised creative solutions to maintain progress despite the overcommitted student schedules. His paddling section is the most complete review of lakes, ponds and rivers in the Berkshire area.

Finally Ben Katz '00 spent numerous hours handling the finishing touches of integrating comments and last minute corrections to carry the project across the finish line, thank you.

Willard Morgan '96
Editor

INTRODUCTION

An infinite number of experiences await you in the North Berkshire area: on Stone Hill or Pine Cobble, in Hopkins Forest, throughout the Taconic or Greylock Ranges or along the Hoosic and Green Rivers. Best of all, these places are right out your door, accessible by foot, bike or a short car ride. Whether you are a student, resident or visitor we encourage you to get out and experience the wonders around you.

The *North Berkshire Outdoor Guide* is a tool to facilitate your relationship with the land. We have designed this book with a progression that first introduces you to the area, basic safety, preparation, and outdoor ethics. Then a series of chapters describes the many easily accessible hiking trails close to Williamstown. Later, you will find information on winter travel, biking, fly-fishing, climbing and paddling.

You need not be an athlete or seasoned outdoor person to explore the region, to experience the regenerative effects of a hike, to read the lessons of the landscape or to encounter those spiritual moments of connection to the earth. Confidently match an activity to your comfort level and gradually increase the challenge over time. Remember to travel lightly, leave only footprints and take only memories.

HOW TO USE THIS BOOK

The *North Berkshire Outdoor Guide* is a resource produced by the Williams Outing Club (WOC) as a service for Williams College students, Williamstown residents and the many North Berkshire visitors the year round. We have made every attempt to present the information in a clear and accessible manner. Please read on to learn how to navigate through the material included in this book.

ABOUT "NORTH BERKSHIRE"
Most guides to this area cover all of Berkshire County or a greater part of Massachusetts. In those publications "North County" usually refers to the Williamstown – North Adams – Mt. Greylock region.

This area is one with specific physiographic boundaries: The Dome to the North, the Taconic Range to the west, the Greylock Range to the south and the Hoosac Range to the east. "North Berkshire" seems an appropriate name for a logically defined area of Berkshire County with outdoor opportunities enough to earn its own guide.

ORGANIZATION
The Table of Contents lists chapter headings to guide you to general information categories such as "What to Bring," "Taconic Range," or "Biking." To find a specific trail or topic, refer to the index. A header on each page helps you find the information you need.

Progressions dominate the organization of information so that the reader can build logically through the book. Early chapters give a history of the area and prepare you to travel with safety, comfort and concern for the environment. Hiking trail descriptions follow, roughly in order of their distance from Williams College.

Other outdoor activities such as winter travel and mountain biking refer to earlier hiking trail descriptions and offer information for areas close to and then far away from campus. The paddling and climbing sections describe locations mostly beyond Williamstown due to a scarcity of local areas.

To further your outdoor knowledge and experience, an extensive Bibliography provides a list of titles and authors to pursue. A collection of Resources gives addresses, phone numbers and web sites of outdoor-related retail stores, local government and non-profit organizations and relevant national organizations.

TRAIL DESCRIPTIONS

The previous edition of this book was exclusively a trail and ski touring guide. Hiking trails remain the core information and fill over half of the text pages. The descriptions are written to be used with the included 15 x 24 inch map, *North Berkshire Trails*. As a result, a local map does not accompany most descriptions. The trails are grouped by geographic region in order of proximity to Williams: Local Walks, Stone Hill, Green Mountain, Taconic Range, The Hopper, Greylock North, Greylock West, Greylock Summit, Greylock East and Greylock South.

For each trail you will see the following information:

TRAIL NAME

Distance: Field checked mileage, rounded to tenths, unless noted "(approximately)." Distances are one-way unless noted otherwise. Many trails may be combined into loops for longer hikes.

Estimated time: A rough estimate of hiking time for an average walking pace, not running, biking or skiing. Times given are one-way, unless indicated otherwise. Expect your times to differ somewhat from this figure. Does not include approach time by car or foot to the trailhead.

Blazes: Indicates the color of paint swatches or plastic pieces on trees to mark the trail.

Map location: A letter and number combination to find the trailhead with an index grid on the *North Berkshire Trails* map.

Maintenance: Name of the organization that maintains the trail. Contact it using information in the Resources section if the trail needs maintenance.

An introductory paragraph mentions points of interest or useful information about the described trail.

HOW TO GET THERE
- Bulleted list of directions with mileage to reach the trailhead.
- All directions begin from Field Park, at the junction of Route 2 and Route 7 in Williamstown.
- Mileage, rounded to tenths and abbreviated, is given as cumulative figures from Field Park unless indicated otherwise.

DESCRIPTION
A route description with mileage (abbreviated mi.) as well as natural history and human history points of interest. Trails closest to Williams College are described in more detail than those distant. **Bold-faced** words are other trails or subjects covered in this guide that may be found through the index. A cross-reference is bolded only the first time it appears in the description. References in *Italics* may be found in the Bibliography.

ACCURACY
Every attempt has been made to provide accurate and complete information about outdoor activities in the North Berkshire area as of January 1999. Thanks to a very active outdoor recreation and land conservation community, new trails are built and old ones rerouted nearly every year. As a result, some information may become outdated. Always heed signs in the field or more current maps. To report changes or corrections, contact:

Williams Outing Club
Attn: Outdoor Guide
1004 Baxter Hall
Williamstown, MA 01267

HOW TO USE THE MAP

North Berkshire Trails has many advantages for outdoor enthusiasts in the Williamstown area. Parts of nine United States Geological Survey (USGS) 7.5 minute quadrangle maps have been combined into one area bounded by mountain ranges. From viewpoints in the area you can see much of the terrain portrayed on the map and identify features that interest you. Icons note trailheads, camping, canoe put-ins and fishing access points. For navigation, magnetic north lines have been printed in magenta and a one kilometer grid facillitates rough distance estimates.

CONTOUR LINES

If you are unfamiliar with topographic maps and contour lines, don't worry. You can use the other information at first and gradually learn how to read the elevation data to improve your navigation skills. A contour line (gray on this map) traces equal elevations along a hillside, as if water filled the valley to that level. A contour interval of 18 meters, approximately 60 feet vertically, separates each line. Practiced map readers can visualize a landscape from the squiggly mass of lines. If you are not there yet, at least use contours to determine the steepness of a route.

Think of a staircase with, let us say, 18 centimeter (about 8 inch) steps, one hundredth the height of our contour line steps. If the steps are far apart you have a gentle grade, maybe in a landscaped garden. On the other hand, if they are close together the stairs go straight up; envision the Mayan pyramids in Central America. Contour lines are like steps: when they are spaced apart (in broad valleys) you will have a gentle grade and when they are tight together (on hillsides), expect a steep climb.

USE OF METRIC

You will notice the metric contours and one kilometer index grid spacing. The USGS has switched to the metric system and WOC has followed that lead for consistency. To avoid confusion for those not used to the metric system, all distances in the text are given in English units: feet, yards or miles, and the map includes a miles scale. Most high points are labelled with metric and English elevation measurements. If you wish to figure another elevation, use the 18-meter contour interval to determine your position and multiply by 3.3 for a rough estimate. The table below will help you with quick conversions.

Meters	Feet	Meters	Feet
138	453	624	2047
156	512	642	2106
174	571	660	2165
192	630	678	2225
210	689	696	2284
228	748	714	2343
246	807	732	2402
264	866	750	2461
282	925	768	2520
300	984	786	2579
318	1043	804	2638
336	1102	822	2697
354	1161	840	2756
372	1220	858	2815
390	1280	876	2874
408	1339	894	2933
426	1398	912	2992
444	1457	930	3051
462	1516	948	3110
480	1575	966	3169
498	1634	984	3229
516	1693	1002	3288
534	1752	1020	3347
552	1811	1038	3406
570	1870	1056	3465
588	1929	1074	3524
606	1988	1092	3583

INDEX GRID

Each trail description includes a "Map location" coordinate such as "L – 12" to find the trailhead. A grid of letters from east to west and numbers from north to south allows you to locate places within a one-kilometer square on *North Berkshire Trails*.

ACCURACY

All the elevation data and most political information (roads, buildings, etc.) derive from USGS topographical maps. Trails highlighted in yellow have been field checked for accuracy and many were carefully surveyed for an exact location. Many features you find in the field, such as logging roads, may not be indicated on the map. At this scale of 1:50,000 we have shown only the most important information and left off other features to avoid clutter and improve readability. Never rely solely on this map as truth, use all your powers of observation to reconcile any discrepancies you find in the field.

THE WILLIAMS OUTING CLUB

W hen I went to college, I met for the first time with mountain scenery and it has yielded to me...the most skill-
fully concocted cup of physical and spiritual pleasures I have
ever found anywhere in life.

John Bascom

HISTORY

In 1793 Williams College students lived in isolation from the outside world. The North Berkshire area legitimately constituted a
sphere of its own and those living here knew the landscape well.
Simple travel and work on foot or horse along narrow paths, carriage roads or wood grades brought students and townspeople into
close contact with the land every day. Mountain Day, an annual
holiday from classes starting in the early 19th century, freed students to explore the North Berkshire Hills or "Purple Valley".

In 1830 Williams students and professors led a crew of one hundred who cleared the Hopper Trail, three miles from Haley Farm
to the summit of Mt. Greylock, in one day. That year students also
built a wooden tower on the summit for sightseeing and scientific
observation, which was rebuilt and maintained into the 1850's.

Growing appreciation of mountains for their own sake found
direction in the Alpine Club, founded in 1863 by professor Albert
Hopkins. This was the first mountain climbing organization in the
United States, before the White Mountain Club (1873) or Appalachian Mountain Club (1876). The Alpine Club stated its purpose:

To explore the interesting places in the vicinity; to become
better aquainted...with the natural history of the localities, and
to improve the pedestrian powers of the members.

The Club produced newsletters, wrote trip journals and named many
features of the North Berkshire Hills.

A student government committee on "trails and byways" was organized in 1904, and a small group of undergraduates founded the current Williams Outing Club (WOC). WOC devoted its early years to winter sports, capturing the intercollegiate winter sports title in 1925, and encouraging interest in winter sports amongst Williams students in general.

In 1923, WOC took charge of the annual Winter Carnival, a major enterprise still organized and staffed by students. Held each February, the carnival includes alpine and nordic ski races, a snow sculpture contest with faculty judges and an array of campus events. For several years the club ran an ice skating rink on Eph's Pond and a ski area at Sheep Hill, complete with three trails, a warming hut and a 35-meter jump.

By 1927, the club had expanded its scope to include mainte-nance of hiking trails, intending to "open up all the previously neglected footpaths about Williamstown in order that those who so desire may tramp about the foothill." The first edition of the WOC Trail Guide, *The Mountains of Eph*, was published that sum-mer.

To facilitate longer hiking and backpacking trips, WOC built several different cabins and shelters; the first was the Harris Me-morial Cabin, located between Mount Williams and Mount Fitch (1932), but only a chimney remains today. Currently, the club maintains a cabin in Hopkins Forest, a 2425-acre educational and research facility owned by Williams College, as well as a lean-to near the tri-state border.

After decades of faithfully serving the college community through trails and winter sports, WOC has wildly expanded its definition of the word "outing" in the latter part of this century to organize activities ranging from kayaking to rock climbing to con-tra dancing.

WOC has also broadened its role as a service organization in the Williams College and Williamstown community. Members teach physical education classes where fellow students learn new out-door skills and the instructors develop their teaching and leader-ship abilities. Others organize a slate of day and overnight trips in the North Berkshires and throughout New England.

Each September, WOC runs the Williams Outdoor Orientation to Living as First-Years (WOOLF), a program that provides preorientation outdoor trips from two to five days long for new students. To demonstrate the unparalleled mountain access of Williamstown, the majority of trips begin hiking from campus.

Members (limited to the Williams College community) support WOC with an annual fee. Those who want to explore the Williamstown area on their own can borrow a wide variety of equipment from the Equipment Room and use resources in the Reading Room. WOC is also responsible for the upkeep and supervision of the popular 2000 square foot Nate Lowe Memorial Climbing Wall opened in 1995.

Few colleges have such a natural bounty of outdoor opportunities out their front door. The Williams Outing Club stands on the shoulders of Williams students who, since 1793, have plied the hills first by necessity, for study or for pleasure. WOC has evolved from Professor Hopkins' Alpine Club and a small group of students promoting winter sports, to a large organization that encompasses more than a third of the student body and a wide range of outdoor activities. Despite the inevitable changes of time, the mission of WOC remains true to the ideals of the Alpine Club 135 years ago:

> …To stimulate participation and appreciation for outdoor activities…To further the ideal of college education, develop personal initiative and leadership, promote skills in outdoor recreation, educate itself and the college community about environmental conservation, seek new opportunities for outreach, and encourage the meeting of people with common interests.

WOC Constitution

MOUNTAIN DAY

Mountains of Eph, the first edition of the WOC Trail Guide, described Mountain Day as,

> That day set apart by the Faculty to give the students the opportunity of becoming better acquainted with the mountains in the glory of the autumn foliage.

Today hikes and bike trips from a variety of points converge at Stony Ledge, a rocky outcropping high above the Hopper. Several hundred Williams students, faculty and staff members typically attend the festivities that include refreshments and musical entertainment by campus groups. From Stony Ledge the Greylock Range from Mt. Prospect to Mt. Greylock and Saddleball Mountain show off their vibrant colors.

The origin of Mountain Day is believed to date back to the early years of Williams when a day known as "Chip Day" was set aside each spring for students to clear the debris left over from the cutting and splitting of firewood during the winter. When Chip Day arrived in 1796, students subscribed to a fund and employed others to clean up for them. Freed from their task, they took the day as a holiday and spent it as they pleased.

Although Williams observed Chip Day throughout the first half of the nineteenth century, an additional holiday, soon known as Mountain Day, was granted so that students could go to the mountains, especially Mt. Greylock. The first recorded reference to Mountain Day is in President Edward Dorr Griffin's journal for 1827.

Student interest waxed during the mid 19th Century and the College instituted "Bald Mountain Day" (the original name of Stony Ledge) as well in 1857, when students first celebrated fall foliage from Stony Ledge. The Chapel chimes announced Mountain Day with the college's alma mater, "The Mountains," through the late 19th and early 20th century while interest waned. Among other activities, WOC always sponsored an overnight trip up Mt. Greylock.

In 1934, Mountain Day was officially abolished due to lack of interest–only 40 students had participated the year before. Faculty members were afraid that if they gave students the day off, they would spend it in ways other than enjoying the outdoors.

By the 1960s, students began to advocate the resurrection of Mountain Day. A 1969 Williams Record editorial argued that such a holiday would "focus attention on our surroundings, which seem to go unnoticed by so many students." Williams finally resumed the celebration of Mountain Day in 1981. While students are no longer given the day off from classes, Mountain Day still encourages the Williams community to get outside and appreciate the beauty of the "Purple Hills" in fall.

ORIGINS OF PLACE NAMES

Adams .... After statesman and Revolutionary War hero Samuel Adams.

Bennington .... For Governor Benning Wentworth of New Hampshire.

Berkshires .... Named for a county in England, where the name is pronounced "Bark-sheer." A "shire" is an anglo-saxon administration district

Fitch, Mt. .... For Ebenezer Fitch the first president of Williams College.

Green Mountains ..... From the French "Vert mont" which means green mountain. This is also the derivation of the state of Vermont.

Green River .... Probably given because of the characteristic color of the water.

Greylock, Mt. .... There are many versions of the story of how this mountain got its name. Some believe that it was named for Waranoce, a Native American chief from Maine who was called Gray Lock by the early settlers. Many historical references to the wisps of cloud that often shroud the summit and its "hoary aspect in winter" by writers and Williams College professors provide a more likely origin of the name.

Hoosic .... Derived from the Mohican Indian words "wujoo," meaning "a mountain," and "abic," meaning "a rock." The mountain range is spelled "Hoosac," the city

"Hoosick," and the river "Hoosic."

Hopper .... Named for its resemblance to a grain hopper.

Hopkins Forest .... After Amos Lawrence Hopkins, whose farm covered most of what is now the Massachusetts portion of the forest.

New Ashford .... For the "new ash fort" constructed on the Cheshire to Williamstown stage road in 1750.

Pittsfield .... Named for Sir William Pitt, the English statesman who befriended the colonies. His birthday coincides with the day in April 1761 that Berkshire County split off from Hampshire County.

Stone Hill .... Refers to the quartzite outcrops once visible in many places from the valley below.

Taconic .... Either from the Indian names Taagh-ka-nick, meaning "water enough," or Tach-an-ni-ke, meaning "full of timber."

Williams, Mt. .... Named for Williams College and Ephraim Williams.

Williamstown .... Named for Colonel Ephraim Williams, who willed his fortune to the town of West Hoosak to found a free school (Williams College), on the condition that the name be changed to Williamstown.

STARTING OUT

Common sense will take you a long way in the outdoors. Remember that you are responsible for your own safety, warmth, water, food and shelter. The lack of modern amenities to provide those basic needs makes the outdoors so compelling.

For a short walk to Eph's Pond you have little to think about, maybe an extra layer of clothing in the fall. On a couple–mile hike of Pine Cobble you will expend a bit more energy and climb in elevation where weather may be different. A small pack with water, a snack and a layer may suffice. An all day trip on Greylock requires a few more items, a multi-day backpack trip even more.

If you are new to the mountains, be conservative at first; let the simple information herein guide you, then seek out more information on organized trips or through literature referenced in the Bibliography. As you become accustomed to the Berkshire Hills let experience, knowledge and fitness govern your judgements of what to bring. The old Boy Scout motto of "Be Prepared" does not mean you must have a mountain of "gear" on your back. Quite the contrary, be prepared with common sense, experience, sound knowledge and a basic amount of equipment adjusted to the season as well as length and intensity of the excursion.

Most important, get out there and have fun. One thirsty or hungry trek will encourage you to bring water or food the next time. Experience will teach you more than any words in a book.

SAFETY

To avoid an "experience" of dangerous proportions, here are a few basic safety guidelines to follow. Always tell someone where you are going, especially if you go alone. If no friends are around, leave a note; that small gesture can save hours if you need assistance. Keep in mind how far you are from help and take responsibility for your own safety. A badly sprained ankle on Pine Cobble could mean a lengthy ordeal.

Adjust to the season and check the weather when possible; storms may sweep in quickly to change conditions dramatically. From late October to mid December a series of hunting seasons in Massachusetts, Vermont and New York make travel in the hills dangerous. Call the Outing Club or Department of Fisheries and Wildlife for dates and information.

Please be careful if you are driving to a trailhead; that is the most dangerous part of your trip. Finally, keep aware toward the end of your trip when fatigue and eagerness to finish may cause an accident or lapse in judgement.

WHAT TO WEAR

Season, weather, the activity and your intensity all affect how to dress on a given day. A "layer" system with attention to the fabric types can make any trip a pleasure, whether hot and dry or cold and wet.

Heat (or lack thereof), wetness, and wind are the major factors that govern how to dress comfortably. Heat may emanate from the sun or your own body, precipitation and sweat introduce moisture and wind causes evaporation and convective cooling.

Different fabrics offer various degrees of insulation, water repellency, and wind protection. A material insulates by trapping air in spaces either made by a weave or existing between layers. To protect against precipitation, a garment must have holes no bigger than a raindrop. To accomplish this purpose a fabric may be coated or laminated with a membrane that has microscopic pores. Waterproofed seams complete your rain protection. A tightly woven or lightly coated material may effectively block wind, but might not be waterproof.

Cotton is comfortable and insulates fairly well, but only when dry. When wet, all the air spaces collapse and convective cooling takes over. On a hot summer day, that feels great, but in winter cotton earns the title "death cloth."

Wool fibers retain a coating of oil that allow them to resist water saturation and maintain air spaces to insulate. For most of history, wool was the fabric of choice for outdoor activity during inclement weather.

However, since the early 1980's polyester and other synthetic fabrics have become the standard of outdoor clothing. Essentially plastic, a petroleum product, synthetic fibers resist moisture and insulate when wet, much like wool. Unlike wool, synthetics are not scratchy and may be customized into a myriad of products.

Informed layering can make any weather conditions manageable. The key is to regulate your body temperature, not too warm and not too cold. Aggressively vent by opening zippers or rolling up sleeves and remove or add layers as necessary. Ideally, you learn how to adjust before you become hot or cold.

During cold weather wetness is your greatest enemy, usually in the form of sweat. To avoid overheating, start cold; take off a layer before moving and your body will quickly warm up. Before you begin to sweat, vent and de-layer. At a rest break, quickly put on a jacket and hat to stay warm and remove them before starting again.

Below is more information about a standard layering system for all but warm summer days.

Next to the skin layer	Long underwear. Synthetics wick moisture away from your skin and insulate when wet. No cotton!
Insulating layer(s)	Fleece or wool shirt, sweater or jacket. Adjust thickness or number of layers to weather.
Shell	Windproof and water-resistant at least. Waterproof best. There are many options so shop around. Waterproof/breathable works best, stops rain but water vapor from your body goes out (mostly).

You can layer your torso, lower body, feet, hands and head individually. If you don't have a lot of fancy wool or synthetic clothes, work with what you have, but realize you have to be much more diligent to avoid sweating and losing your insulation.

FOOTWEAR

As with clothing and equipment, adjust your footwear to the demands of an activity. Sneakers or even sandals are fine for local walks. Once on mountain trails, boots offer greater foot and ankle protection. Lightweight leather and fabric models are fine for most hikes. On an overnight trip, stiffer boots reduce the likelihood of spraining an ankle with a heavy pack. In winter, insulated or double boots keep your feet warm and dry.

Beware of new boots, which often don't fit properly, or need to be broken in. Try to break in new boots BEFORE heading out into the woods by wearing them around town. Wear two pairs of socks: a smooth liner sock and a thick wool sock to reduce friction and blisters. If you feel a "hot spot" from rubbing, stop, adjust your socks and lacing or put on moleskin to prevent a blister. On an overnight trip, bring a pair of comfortable camp shoes to relax in.

HYDRATION

Drink water, and lots of it. A field measure of adequate hydration is "clear and copious," regarding your urine. On an overnight trip that means between three and five quarts per day, more for high exertion or winter activities. Proper hydration helps body temperature regulation, food metabolism and muscle endurance. Carry at least one full water bottle on any excursion.

WHAT TO BRING

Your brain is the most important tool in the outdoors! Remember "common sense" too and bring plenty of it. If you are reading this information, you are on the right track; a few basic tips can short-cut a long learning curve of mistakes. Below is a series of equipment lists for trips relating to the trails described in this guide. Items with an asterisk * are available in the WOC Equipment Room for WOC members.

Local Walks
- Weather-appropriate clothing (see What to Wear).
- Extra layer – Sweater, fleece or windbreaker. *

Short Hikes – Stone Hill, Hopkins Forest, Pine Cobble, etc.
- All items for Local Walks plus...
- Full water bottle. *
- Snack.
- Small daypack or hip pack. *
- Trail guide and map. *

Half Day Hikes – Dome, Hopper, Taconic Range trails.
- All items for Short Hikes plus…
- Extra food.
- Sun protection – Hat, sunscreen and sunglasses.
- Pocketknife – A thousand uses.
- Rain gear – Even on a sunny day. *
- Compass – If you know how to use one. *
- Flashlight or headlamp – Just in case. *
- First aid supplies. *
- Hiking boots (see Footwear).
- Thick wool or synthetic blend socks.

Full Day Hikes – Mt. Greylock, loops with several trails.
- All items for Half Day Hikes plus…
- Second full water bottle. *
- Lunch.
- More first aid supplies. *
- Whistle – For emergency.
- Hat and gloves – Essential any time of year.
- Small tarp – To sit on or for an emergency shelter.

Overnight – Anywhere in the area or beyond.
- All items for Full Day Hikes plus…
- Extra socks – Keep feet warm and dry.
- Backpack – Internal or external frame. *
- Sleeping bag – Appropriate temperature rating. *
- Sleeping pad – Insulates you from cold ground. *
- Shelter – Tent, tarp or bivy sack. *
- Camp shoes – Sandals or old running shoes.
- Ground tarp – Under tent or sleeping pad.*
- Food – See below.
- Stove – Fires are restricted in most areas.*
- Fuel – Appropriate to stove. *
- Matches or lighter.*
- Cooking pot. *
- Pot grips – To avoid burning skin or clothes. *

Overnight (continued)
- Cup, bowl and spoon. *
- Toilet paper and trowel – See Sanitation. *
- Toiletries – Toothbrush and toothpaste.
- Trash bags – To keep clothes dry.
- Rope – To hang food away from animals. *
- Camera.
- Journal.

Winter
- All items for Day-Hike or Overnight plus…
- Mittens, shell mittens or both.
- Balaclava or neck gaiter.
- Liner socks – Reduce moisture, help insulate.
- Gaiters – Keep snow out of boots. *
- Layer clothing system (See above).
- Wool sock to insulate water bottle.
- Thermos is nice.
- Down or synthetic-fill jacket helpful.

FOOD

"I think," said Christopher Robin, "that we ought to eat all our
provisions now, so we won't have so much to carry."

A. A. Milne

Common sense extends to fueling your body during sustained outdoor activity. For a short hike, grab a piece of fruit or a granola
bar. On long day and overnight trips, the primary guideline is to
eat a lot. Your body may not be used to so much exertion or the
demands of weather. Always pack a little extra food, just in case
something unexpected happens. In the winter, it is a great idea to
carry a hot drink with lots of sugar in it, in case you need to warm
people up!

The most important factors to consider when selecting food for an extended trip are energy content, weight, preparation time and taste. Below is a list of useful staples and ingredients to help you decide what to take. Before leaving, repackage as much food as possible in sturdy plastic or Ziploc® bags, in order to minimize weight, volume and the amount of garbage you will have to carry out with you. Try snacking all day on the trail instead of eating a big lunch, your body will thank you. On short trips you can carry less dried foods. Be creative!

Snacks	Granola bars, fruit, dried fruit, energy bars, nuts, trail mix (peanuts, raisins, nuts, chocolate chips, etc.), chocolate, fig newtons.
Lunch	Bagels, pita bread, tortillas, crackers, peanut butter, almond butter, jam, cream cheese, humus mix, cheese, carrots, pepperoni, tuna.
Breakfast	Hot cereal, cold cereal, dried milk, potato flakes, powdered eggs, pancake mix, dried fruit.
Dinner	Pasta, sauce mixes, rice, beans or bean flakes, couscous, fresh vegetables (onion, pepper, cabbage, carrots best), cheese, soup mix, sun-dried tomatoes, sunflower seeds
Dessert	No-bake cheese cake, pudding (shake to mix in Tupperware® or water bottle), cookies
Extras	Spices (salt, pepper, fresh garlic, oregano, basil, cumin, curry, cinnamon, brewers yeast), hot sauce, salsa, cooking oil, soy sauce, butter or margarine, baking mix, honey, cocoa, tea, drink mix with vitamin C.

For more ideas about backcountry cooking and nutrition refer to the *NOLS Cookery*.

OUTDOOR TRAVEL

You are at the trailhead, maybe for a long day hike or perhaps an overnight trip. A note with your itinerary is at home while a pack with water, food, clothes and some odds and ends hangs on your back. But you have a few questions: What do two paint marks on a tree mean? Should I take this short-cut trail up the steep hill? I wonder what those high clouds mean? Where should I camp? How about a fire? What if I sprain my ankle? What should I do about that trash along the trail? Uh-oh, I need to go to the bathroom.

An explosion in outdoor recreation has led to signs of human presence everywhere, often to the detriment of an experience. The stewardship of natural places is a responsibility of all who use them. One manifestation of this stewardship is a nationwide program named "Leave No Trace." Government agencies and private organizations together promote this program of minimum impact travel in the outdoors. We encourage you to minimize your impact whenever you travel in the North Berkshires and translate that ethic to other areas of your life. That does not mean you must tiptoe through a fragile world. Instead use your brain, that most important tool, to decide how to mitigate your impact.

This section is designed to help you explore the outdoors safely, responsibly and with great fun. The information below is only an introduction, not a comprehensive how-to manual. Refer to titles in the bibliography such as *Soft Paths* or *Leave No Trace* for a more complete description of outdoor travel. While your safety takes precedence over concerns about the environment, good preparation should keep you from having to choose between the two.

HIKING

Most of the time we spend outdoors finds us walking, running, or riding on trails. To help prevent erosion and preserve the beauty of the landscape, avoid widening trails if at all possible. If the ground is muddy, wear waterproof boots and plow through the mud. If it's rocky, don't seek a smooth path alongside the worn trail. Tempting as it may be in some situations, do not cut switchbacks or start other shortcuts of your own.

When you are estimating the mileage you can cover keep the fitness level of your group and the nature of the terrain in mind. Accidents tend to happen when people are traveling at an uncomfortable pace or at the end of a day. Know when it gets dark, and select your starting time with that in mind. Keep your speed consistent and stay together. If you spread out, be sure to stop and regroup at all trail junctions to avoid separating.

Besides using existing footpaths, traveling off trail is also an option in some places. Backcountry areas are often the most rewarding to explore, but you should visit them only if you are confident in your navigation skills and your ability to minimize your ecological impact.

If you are traveling off-trail with a large number of people, plan to hike in parties of not more than six, and choose your route carefully to avoid fragile terrain and critical wildlife habitat. The most durable surfaces for traveling are rock, gravel and sand, which you can usually find along rivers and streams. When hiking on vegetation that will recover from mild trampling, spread out across the hillside; but if the vegetation is fragile, walk single-file to minimize the amount of damage created by your footsteps.

During winter, frozen ground and snow cover dramatically reduce your impact. However, the spring thaw brings sloppy mud and a limit to low impact off-trail travel.

NAVIGATION

That most important tool comes into play again. Above all, be alert and observant when travelling in the outdoors. Make mental notes of notable landmarks, changes in terrain, junctions with old wood roads, a cascading waterfall or a beautiful hemlock grove. Every once in a while, look behind you, a place can be unrecognizable from another angle three hours later. If you are observant, you should at least be able to return the way you came.

To follow a particular route, use the tools available. Carry a trail guide and at least one map of the area. Learn how to read a topographic map and then to use a compass. Familiarize yourself and your group with the route you will be taking, as well as the locations of the nearest road and telephone should you need them. While you are on the trail, be sure to check your map periodically, so you will know where you last were if the group gets lost. Nearly all the trails in this guide are marked with painted or plastic color blazes on trees to help you follow the route. A double blaze, one above the other, marks a turn in the trail. Most trail junctions have signs, but always check your map to be sure a sign has not moved due to weather.

WEATHER

> If you don't like the weather in New England, wait five minutes.
>
> Mark Twain

While this frequently quoted pronouncement is somewhat of an exaggeration, weather in the Berkshires can be quite variable, particularly at higher elevations. In general, winters are warmer and summers are cooler than in areas to the south and east. Check a forecast before you go out, especially for an overnight or winter trip. While out there, stay alert for signs of a change in weather. High thin clouds signal the passage of a front within the next twenty-four hours and a strong wind often precedes a warm or cold front.

Berkshire County Weather	(413) 528-1118
New England Weather Associates	(413) 499-2627
24-hour weather phone	
Berkshire/New England Ski Phone	(413) 499-7669
The Weather Channel	www.weather.com

FIRST AID

The three most important rules for wilderness first aid are prevention, prevention and prevention. Be sure to read the section "Starting Out" for information on appropriate equipment to bring and other preventative considerations. Generally, be conservative when in any risky situations and stay well fed and hydrated. Injuries and medical emergencies in the outdoors are more serious because hospital care may be hours away. Thankfully, emergencies are rare and more often we encounter cuts, blisters, dehydration, fatigue, mild hypothermia or sprains.

Common sense can help you treat these minor conditions on short hikes until you get home. On overnight trips you will want to have more knowledge from reading (see Bibliography) or a first aid course. The Red Cross offers first aid courses in most communities. If you plan to spend a lot of time in the outdoors consider taking a wilderness medicine course offered by organizations such as Solo or Wilderness Medical Associates (see Resources).

If you do have an emergency situation, above all, stay calm and do not create a second victim through haste or carelessness. Administer first aid as you have learned or been trained and go for help. If you have enough people, do not leave the patient alone and have more than one runner leave to call for assistance.

EMERGENCY PHONE NUMBERS

For a life-threatening emergency in Vermont and Massachusetts call **911**.
For a non life-threatening emergency, call one of the following numbers:
- Williamstown Police Department (413) 458-5733
- North Adams Police Department (413) 664-4944
- North Adams Regional Hospital (413) 663-3701
- Berkshire Medical Center (413) 447-2000

Williams College students can call Williams College Security for a non life-threatening emergency at 597-4444. Ask them to get in touch with the Williams Outing Club.

CAMPING

A night outdoors requires a bit more planning than a simple day hike does, but the rewards are great. Refer to the "Starting Out" section for information on clothing, equipment and food. On a night out you become a self-sufficient being with a house on your back, though hopefully one that is not too heavy!

All public lands in the North Berkshire area limit overnight stays to shelters, established tent sites or campgrounds. This policy concentrates impact in specific places to preserve a greater land area. If you travel elsewhere in New England, check local regulations before you go.

While staying at a camp site do all of your washing at least 200 feet from all water sources. Strain dirty dishwater (using an old piece of window screen, cheesecloth, etc.) to remove all food particles, pack these out and scatter the dirty water over a wide area. Hang your food items in a sturdy bag well off the ground to keep animals from getting to them. When you break camp, check the site carefully, pick up any refuse and replace any rocks or ground cover disturbed during your stay. "Pack it in, pack it out" is a motto to keep in mind, and take the time to pack out any trash you find along the way. The next person will appreciate your efforts.

FIRES

What is more enjoyable than a warm campfire after a taxing day on the trail? Campfires – once as much a part of the outdoor experience as sore feet – are now discouraged for a number of reasons. Carelessly built fires leave blackened scars on the forest floor, lessen the soil's ability to hold moisture, and burn away nutrients essential for plant growth. If you are camping in an area where no fires have been built before, you should not build one unless it is absolutely necessary. Carry a camp stove and adequate fuel for cooking your food, as well as enough warm clothing to prevent you from having to rely on a blaze for warmth.

If you are camping in an area where fires are permitted and you do decide to build one, use preexisting fire rings or Leave No Trace techniques. Books such as *Soft Paths* describe how to build a low impact mound fire. Collect only pieces of wood that can be broken by hand and do not break dead branches off standing trees. Do your wood gathering before dark, so that you can locate areas that have not been picked clean by other travelers and avoid trampling vegetation unnecessarily.

WATER

Although the 1927 edition of this guide noted that, "Any of the springs and brooks up in the mountains about Williamstown are safe for drinking purposes," this is no longer the case. Drinking unpurified water may lead to ailments such as giardia, an intestinal illness that causes intense and unpleasant bowel problems. If you cannot bring sufficient water with you, the safest approach is to treat all water before drinking it. Water can be purified through several methods.

> Boiling - Unless you are at a very high elevation, the water is safe to drink as soon as it comes to a rolling boil.
> Iodine or chlorine tablets.
> Commercial filters available in most outdoor stores.

Throughout your trip, make sure that you and everyone with you drinks water constantly. Making sure that you stay properly hydrated can prevent many common backcountry ailments. Three to five quarts a day is the minimum recommended to replace lost fluids. Drink enough to make your urine clear and copious.

SANITATION AND WASTE DISPOSAL

You should be prepared to carry out everything you carry in, including paper, plastic, metal and food scraps. Plan ahead by repackaging food to cut down on waste and bringing trash bags that you can seal shut. Make it a habit to pick up any trash that you see, whether or not it is yours.

When you relieve yourself in the woods, there are some definite dos and don'ts. Urine is mostly water and salts, quite benign to the environment. Feces, on the other hand, can transmit waterborne diseases such as giardia, caused by a protozoan. Human waste should be disposed of in a way that reduces aesthetic and environmental impacts.

Urinate off of trails and away from campsites. Most public lands in the Williamstown area have outhouses at shelters and campgrounds, use them when possible. When there is no outhouse for feces, dig a small hole about six inches deep (in the organic soil) at least 200 feet from water, trails, and campsites. Bring a trowel or improvise a tool, such as your boot heel or a stick to excavate a hole. Avoid gullies that may fill with water in the next heavy rainfall.

After use, stir in some soil with a stick to facilitate fecal decomposition, and cover with soil and duff. If possible, avoid traditional toilet paper and experiment with natural objects like leaves, smooth stones or snow. If you must use toilet paper, note that it decomposes too slowly to bury, and burning it increases the risk of forest fires. Instead carry it out in a sealed plastic bag, and please do not leave little white "flags" to mark your spot.

PUBLIC LANDS AND REGULATIONS

The following are general guidelines for the principal areas described in this guidebook. Since specific regulations change frequently, it is best to call or write for updated information before heading out.

Appalachian Trail
- Fires permitted at official campsites and shelters only.
- Dispersed camping (no fires) allowed in designated areas.
- All vehicles prohibited, including mountain bikes.

Green Mountain National Forest
- Dispersed camping and fires permitted at hiker's discretion.
- Permits required only for commercial groups.

Greylock Reservation, Clarksburg State Forest and Taconic Trail State Park
- No camping or fires allowed in the Hopper, except dispersed camping area near the trailhead.
- Camping allowed elsewhere <u>only</u> in campground areas and shelters on a "first come, first serve" basis. As of February 1998, group sites are available by reservation at 877-I-CAMP-MA.
- No alcoholic beverages.
- Mountain biking on designated trails only.

Hopkins Memorial Forest
- No camping or fires of any kind allowed, although all WOC members are welcome to make use of the Outing Club cabin.
- All vehicles, including mountain bikes, prohibited.
- To obtain a permit for group use and/or collection of any natural material, contact the Center for Environmental Studies at Williams College.

NATURAL HISTORY

A hike in the North Berkshires may be more than just an exercise of the legs, and a journey from a trailhead to a summit. If you exercise your powers of observation, you can also learn something about how the area has come to look the way it does. Natural history includes every aspect of the study of the landscape, from minute details like ant dispersal of seeds from spring flowers to grand events like the advance of glacial ice sheets. Knowing how to read signs of forest succession, tracking animals through fresh snow and understanding the forces that shaped the mountains can help us expand our knowledge and use of the outdoors.

GEOLOGY

The Berkshire Hills are part of the Appalachian Mountain Range, an old mountain system of North America. Between 500 and 250 millions years ago (difficult to imagine) three collisions between North America and other land masses, such as Africa, built mountain ranges that may have been as massive as the modern Rocky Mountains. The intense heat and pressure of these collisions metamorphosed (cooked) the involved rock into new forms.

Common rocks of the North Berkshires are all metamorphic. Marble, formerly limestone, underlies the Hoosic River valley. Quartzite, formerly sandstone, is in scattered locations such as Stone Hill and Pine Cobble. Phyllite and schist, formerly silt and mudstone, compose much of the Taconic, Greylock and Hoosac Ranges. As mountains formed, erosion gradually wore down the landscape over time and water carried sand and silt to the oceans.

Ice ages have come and gone numerous times in "recent" geologic history, measured in millions of years! The last ice age completely covered New England as far south as Long Island and Nantucket only 20,000 years ago. As ice retreated northward through the North Berkshires about 14,500 years ago it dammed the Hoosic River and formed a giant body of water, Lake Bascom. This lake filled the entire valley to an elevation of 1,045 feet, almost 500 feet deep in places! Within 500 years the ice and lake were gone and vegetation returned, to mature in response to gradual global warming over thousands of years.

SETTLEMENT AND SUCCESSION

The next significant change in the landscape of Berkshire County came at the hands of white settlers. By the 1830, over seventy percent of the woods surrounding Williamstown had been logged or cleared for farming. With the opening of Erie Canal in 1825, however, the poorer farmers began moving West in search of more productive land and abandoned their fields, while the more prosperous farmers remained and bought up the land. Eventually they gave way to the processes of forest succession.

This ecological cycle begins with the colonization of open areas by fastest-growing, fast-dispersing "pioneer" species, a group that in this region is dominated by "puckerbrush", a tangled thicket of shrubs and young trees. Eventually, hardier and more shade-tolerant species appear among the aging colonizers. The seedlings of the colonizers cannot withstand the increased shade, so as the older individuals die, they fail to replace themselves. Over time, this produces a shift from flash-in-the-pan colonizers to slower-growing but longer-lived species.

Today, although you can see the foundations of old farmhouses and crumbling stone walls in many formerly cultivated areas, seventy five percent of the regional landscape is again covered with trees.

FLORA AND FAUNA

Above 2,500 feet boreal forests of mostly red spruce and balsam fir dominate because of more severe weather conditions. At most lower elevations, deciduous forests reign. The most common trees on the north and east facing slopes are sugar maple, beech, yellow birch, white birch and hemlock. On south and west facing slopes, oaks and hickory are prevalent. However, relative abundance of various species may differ as a result of a wide variety of factors, including the land use history of a particular area.

Red maple dominates former pastureland, paper birch and bigtooth aspen favor areas once used for growing crops, and rows of red oaks can often be found along the edges of abandoned carriage roads and woodlots. The presence of longer-lived species like beech, sugar maple and hemlock, in terms of succession, represent a stand in their climax stages, which can also be distinguished by a much more diverse range of tree sizes and ages.

Northern hardwoods provide the spectacular display of fall colors that attract visitors from all over the country. In the spring and summer, they also harbor a number of stunning wildflowers, particularly the early-blooming spring ephemerals, which bloom and wither before the trees leaf out.

Common mammals in the Williamstown area include white-tail deer, eastern gray squirrels, red squirrels, eastern chipmunks, eastern cottontail rabbits, mice, shrews, moles and voles, as well as opossums, woodchucks and porcupines. Those who are on the trail at dawn or dusk may see more wildlife and less common species such as gray foxes. Rare mammals include bobcat and river otters.

Reforestation has brought an increase in the population of both black bears and coyotes. Neither poses a serious danger to people; they generally flee at the sight or smell of humans, but coyotes can be a threat to small domestic animals. Keep your eyes open to see what you find out there.

For more information refer to *Farms to Forest*, *North Woods*, *Eastern Forest*s or other sources listed in the bibliography.

INTRODUCTION TO HIKING

There is something unnatural about walking. Especially uphill, which always seems to me not only unnatural, but so unnecessary. That iron tug of gravitation should be all the reminder we need that in walking uphill we are violating a basic law of nautre...[Yet] there are some good things to say about walking...It stretches time and prolongs life...I have a friend who's always in a hurry; he never gets anywhere. Walking makes the world much bigger, and therefore more interesting. You have time to observe the details...

Edward Abbey

HIKING

An enormous number of hiking trails and old logging roads can be found in the Williamstown area. They include everything from gentle strolls along cool mountain streams, to steep ascents with breathtaking views of the surrounding mountain peaks. For those who want to spend a longer period of time outdoors, there are a variety of shelters and campsites, both accessible and remote. This section focuses on those trails that can be reached on foot or with a drive of fifteen minutes or less. Rather than outlining complete routes, we have chosen to describe individual trails and how they connect with each other, so that you can design your own adventures. A list of some favorite WOC hikes appears on the following pages.

The trail descriptions are divided into sections: **Local Walks, Stone Hill**, **Green Mountain, Taconic** and **Greylock** . The first section and Stone Hill describe a few smaller areas that are located within, or immediately adjacent to the central part of Williamstown. The Green Mountain section covers the area to the north, including a portion of the Appalachian and Long Trails. The Taconic section is comprised of the Taconic Range that stands to the west of Williamstown, and the Greylock section covers the Greylock Range, which is situated to the southeast.. Each description includes directions to the trailhead and an explanation of the route, as well as comments on possibilities for other outdoor recreation like mountain biking and cross-country skiing. There is also a listed "hiking time" for each trail, which is based on the formula used in AMC's <u>White Mountain Guide:</u> one half-hour for every mile of walking, and one half hour for every thousand feet of elevation. Once you have hiked a few trails, and compared your actual hiking times to the listed ones, you should be able to estimate how long it will take you to hike any other trail in the book. Within each chapter, hikes are arranged in order of their proximity to the center of Williamstown.

When setting off on a hike of any length, remember that good preparation is essential for your comfort and safety. Be sure to read the introductory sections of this guide, which deal with issues like first-aid and traveling in the outdoors. Always check the weather before you head out, and leave a copy of your itinerary with friends. Respect your own limits, and those of your group– remember, the mountains will still be there next week or next month. Above all, have fun exploring this extraordinary place!

DEER HUNTING SEASON

If you venture into the woods for any reason during late fall, exercise extreme caution. Wear brightly colored (but not white) clothing and consider carrying a string of bells to jingle as you walk. The most dangerous seasons for hikers are the rifle and shotgun seasons, but it is also important to be aware of the seasons for bow-hunting and muzzle-loaders, which occur around the same time. The approximate dates for local hunting seasons follow:

Massachusetts: Shotgun season–third week in November to
           mid-December.
New York: Rifle season–first Monday after November 15 to
           first Tuesday after December 7.
Vermont: Rifle season–second half of November.
           Muzzle loader season–second week in Decem-
           ber.

For the exact dates of the deer hunting seasons in any given year,
contact WOC or call one of the numbers listed below:

Massachusetts Department of Fish and Wildlife: (413) 447-9789
New York Department of Fish and Wildlife: (518) 457-3730
Vermont Department of Fish and Wildlife: (802) 241-3700

The sixty-odd trail descriptions that follow may be overwhelming
to those new to the North Berkshire area. Here are some recommended hikes to get you started. Enjoy!

SHORT HIKES (less than 4 hours)
  Berlin Mountain (Class of '33) Trail
  Berlin Pass Trail
  Phelps Trail–Taconic Crest Trail–Mill's Hollow Trail
  Hopkins Forest Loop
  Pine Cobble Trail
  Stone Hill Loop Trail
  Overlook–Hopper–Appalachian Trails
  Stony Ledge–Roaring Brook Trails
  Roaring Brook–Circular or Deer Hill Trails

LONGER HIKES (4 hours or more)
  R.R.R. Brooks Trail–Shepherd's Well–Taconic Crest–Birch
  Brook Trails
  Broad Brook–Agawon–Dome Trails
  Pine Cobble–Appalachian–Broad Brook Trails
  Hopper–Money Brook–Mount Prospect Trails
  Old Adams Road–Appalachian–Chesire Harbor Trails

LOCAL WALKS

S everal areas near campus and the commercial district are convenient for a short stroll or a picnic lunch on a warm, sunny day. On each walk you can appreciate the proximity of Williams College and Williamstown to natural places. So put on your shoes and explore. Your car will be useful to reach trails described later.

LINEAR PARK

Distance: Short walk.
Estimated time: 30 minutes or more.
Blazes: Some faded blue.
Map location: I– 18.
Maintenance: Town of Williamstown.

This small park, maintained by the town of Williamstown, is a convenient place to eat a picnic lunch or spend a quiet hour enjoying the outdoors. The Green River, flowing to the Hoosic River, passes through the park.

HOW TO GET THERE
Linear Park may be reached on foot from Spring Street or any location on the Williams Campus via a number of different routes. If you are visiting the park for the first time, or you are in a car, use the following directions.
- Take Route 2 east to Water Street (Route 43).
- Turn right on Water Street, and follow it 0.2 mi. to a bridge over the Green River to the left.
- You will see a sign for the park as you cross the bridge.
- Around the bend to the right is a small graveled parking area with room for 3-4 cars.

DESCRIPTION

At first glance, Linear Park is a grassy area with several picnic tables, two barbecue grills, and a variety of play equipment for children. A short scramble down the slope behind the picnic tables to the Green River and you will find yourself in a different world. Here the noise of flowing water quiets the cars and trucks above, and the cleft of the riverway obscures buildings and pavement. An old path along the river marked with blue blazes connects gravel bars and sculpted phyllite outcrops. Explore and find your own spot to read, study, or watch the water flow by.

A study by the **Hoosic River Watershed Association** in the fall of 1998 found that most of the Green River is now of swimmable/fishable status. Avoid ingesting the water, but cooling off on a hot summer day is safe thanks to local conservation efforts.

EPH'S POND

Distance: Short walk.
Estimated time: Your choice.
Blazes: None.
Map location: I – 20.
Maintenance: Williams College.

Named after Colonel Ephraim Williams, whose bequest started the Free School that became Williams College, Eph's pond is a great place to observe birds or a magnificent view of the ranges surrounding Williamstown.

HOW TO GET THERE

On foot from campus, students walk north, towards Mission Park and the tennis courts, then down Stetson road past the field house and downhill toward Cole Field.

- By car, drive east on Route 2 from Field Park to Park St., the second road on your left (0.2 mi.).
- Turn onto Park, and follow it north 0.3 mi. to Lynde Lane.
- Turn right (east) onto Lynde Ln. (0.5 mi.) and then left (north) on Stetson Road at the tennis courts after 0.1 miles.
- Follow Stetson Rd. to Eph's pond and the playing fields (1.0 mi. total).

• Park to the left, along the barrier. Please do not block the gate or roadway.

DESCRIPTION

The open playing fields of Cole Field allow a 360-degree view of **Pine Cobble** to the east, the **Greylock Range** to the south, the **Taconic Range** to the west, and the **Dome** to the north. Hiking trails lace all of these areas and descriptions follow in later chapters. Refer to the map in this book to aid identification of these areas.

Eph's pond is part of a very altered floodplain area. Nevertheless, wildlife abounds, including over 100 species of birds, numerous amphibians, mammals and reptiles. Refer to *A Guide to Natural Places in the Berkshire Hills* (see bibliography) for more information about the flora and fauna of Eph's pond and the **Hoosic River**.

A warm spring or summer evening is a perfect time to listen to peepers while walking along the edge of Eph's Pond or continue on the Hoosic River. Also, one can sight migratory water-foul in the spring and autumn.

HOOSIC RIVER LOOP TRAIL

Distance: Up to 1.5 miles.
Estimated time: 30 – 60 minutes.
Blazes: None.
Map location: I – 20.
Maintenance: Hoosic River Watershed Association.

Williamstown lies at the confluence of the Green and Hoosic Rivers. Centuries ago, these waterways were the focus of life as sources of water and food and a means of transportation. Later, water powered the early industrial revolution, yet many New England towns turned their backs on local waterways, using them as sewers and dumping grounds, channeling the riverbeds, and building up to the rivers edge. Not until the Clean Water Act in 1972 and new ethics of watershed management did the town begin to clean its formerly life-giving waterways. Still today, the Green and Hoosic Rivers are hidden behind buildings with few access points or trails. Eph's

Pond and Cole Field provide excellent access to the Hoosic within the North Adams–Williamstown corridor.

HOW TO GET THERE
- Refer to directions for Eph's Pond (page 34).

DESCRIPTION
From Eph's Pond, walk north, around a gate and along a paved path towards the Hoosic River and floodplain forest. As the black-top path bears right toward a public restroom and canoe launch, look for a wide grassy path to the left. The woods here are only thirty years old, grown since a landfill on this site closed in 1972. On the left is a ditch where the outlet from Eph's pond empties via a culvert under the playing fields. This area has been severely impacted, yet offers a close look at the Hoosic River and riparian habitat.

Follow the footpath to and along the riverbank. Notice the riprap, concrete blocks and rock lining the banks to prevent erosion and meandering of the river. The Hoosic drains all of north Berkshire and flows north to join the Hudson River in New York. During high water the trail you walk on lies underwater and at flood stage the playing fields may be inundated as well!

Explore the network of side trails on the bank and gravel bars, and head downstream. River otters as well as the occasional bea-ver may be seen along the banks if you are lucky. Due to con-certed efforts in recent decades the Hoosic River is classified as swimable and fishable, but take care and do not drink from the river!

All the paths converge farther downstream. Cross a small foot-bridge and wet swale before entering a clear, grassy area. Ahead is Park St. and Route 7, to return to your car, follow the grassy right of way to the left. A footpath shares the byway with a sewer line to the Williamstown Sewage Treatment plant, located across the Hoosic River to the north.

Each May the **Hoosic River Watershed Association** organizes a celebration called Riverfest to celebrate the Hoosic River. If in town at that time, be sure to check it out.

HOOSIC RIVER NATURE TRAIL

Distance: Less than 0.5 mile.
Estimated time: 20 minutes.
Map location: J – 19.
Blazes: None. Interpretive signs.
Maintenance: Williamstown Rural Lands Foundation and Hoosic
River Watershed Association.

This short interpretive walking trail begins in the historic Mill Village neighborhood of Williamstown. Signs share information about the importance of riparian areas as you walk along the Hoosic and Green Rivers.

HOW TO GET THERE
From campus or Spring Street, an on-foot approach can make this into a pleasant 2-hour walk through town.
- Drive east on Route 2 to the first stop light (0.6 mi.).
- Turn left on Cole Avenue and drive north toward the Hoosic River.
- Before the river, turn right on Arnold St. (1.1 mi.).
- Immediately turn left on Mill Street (one way).
- Follow Mill Street to a sign marking the Nature Trail (1.3 mi.). Park off the road.

DESCRIPTION
Local efforts to improve Hoosic River access led to this interpretive trail on Williamstown land. From the end of Mill Street, walk east down to the Hoosic River floodplain. A footpath follows the right-of-way of the municipal sewer line upstream to the Green River confluence.

You may wander up the Green River towards Route 2, or loop back to Mill Street along the riverside nature trail. Scattered signs along the way have information about the riparian ecosystem.

OTHER WALKS IN WILLIAMSTOWN

You do not need a guidebook to explore the streets of Williamstown. Any time of year you can set out for a stroll along the centuries old roads, many of which follow original footpaths. If you like to run, check out *A Runner's Guide to Williamstown*, available in local bookstores. Below are a few suggested routes to check out, listed from shortest to longer. Use the map in this book, or a Williamstown map to find your way.

Stetson Road to Cole Field to Cole Avenue.
West Main Street to Northwest Hill Road to Bulkley Street.
South Street to Gale or Ide Road .
Route 43 to Blair Road to Stratton Road .

STONE HILL

E arly settlers named Stone Hill for the outcroppings of quartzite that were visible along the ridge when most trees had been cleared from the hill in the 18th century. Geologists speculate that these rocks, now obscured by vegetation, are the solidified and metamorphosed remains of a sandy ocean coastline from about 550 million years ago, formed while the majority of this region was in the tropical latitudes. Since the rock tends to be quite intensely fractured, settlers often used it for building.

Stone Hill is one of the most popular places to walk and hike in the Williamstown area. There are a number of trails that may be combined to form loops of different lengths and difficulty. Described here are the Pasture Loop, Stone Bench Loop, Stone Hill Loop, Stone Hill Road, and Gale Road Cut-off, in that order. The Town of Williamstown, the Clark Art Institute, Williams College and several private landholders own and manage land over which trails pass. Although Stone Hill has long been open to public wandering, please respect postings and private property.

A local map on the next page is an excerpt from the *North Berkshire Trails* map included in the back of this book.

Stone Bench–Found on top of Stone Hill.
Drawing by Mark Livingston'72.

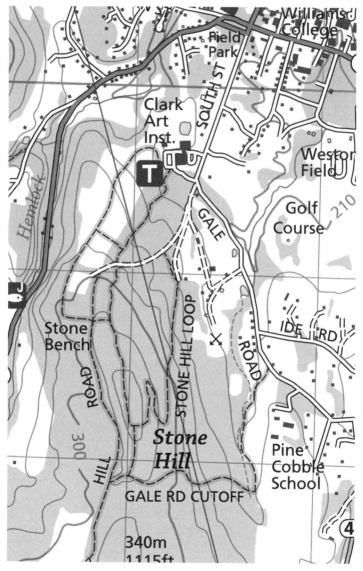

Stone Hill – Local Map.

PASTURE LOOP

Distance: 0.7 miles.
Estimated time: 30 minutes.
Blazes: White diamonds.
Map location: H – 18.
Maintenance: Clark Art Institute and Williams Outing Club.

A wonderful walk to and through the pasture above the Clark Art Institute. Students and townspeople alike return again and again to enjoy the spectacular view of Williamstown, Pine Cobble, and the Dome to the north.

HOW TO GET THERE
- From the intersection of Routes 2 and 7, go south on South Street (opposite Route 7 north).
- After 0.5 mi., turn right into the Clark Art Institute.
- If you are on foot, continue around the building through the grassy area on the left.
- If you are driving, go under the overhead walkway, turn left and park your car in the rear of the parking lot. A sign and two small gravestones mark the trailhead.

DESCRIPTION
The two small gravestones (0.0 mi.) mark the burial place of dogs that belonged to an earlier property owner, Dr. Vanderpool Adriance. The lower portion of this trail, and the footbridge that leads to it, were constructed in 1985 to help celebrate the 30th anniversary of the Clark Art Institute.

Crossing the footbridge (0.1 mi.), the trail winds uphill through a variety of birch, beech and maple stands, as well as some hemlock and pine. At 0.3 mi. a signed trail junction marks the turn-off for the pasture loop to the right. Straight ahead the trail leads to the **Stone Bench Loop, Stone Hill Loop, Stone Hill Road** and **Gale Road Cut-off.**

To continue the pasture loop, turn right and continue to a gate. Pass through the gate being sure to close it behind you. A worn path leads west across the pasture to a grove of trees with excellent views. Grazing cows often dot the pasture and may glance at you, but pose no threat to your safety. To return to the Clark Art Institute below, follow a worn grassy double track downhill on the far side of the field, through a hedgerow and either right or straight to gates in the fence (0.7 mi.). Again, please close the gates behind you.

STONE BENCH LOOP

Distance: 1.5 miles.
Estimated time: 1 hour.
Blazes: White diamond (shared with Pasture Loop) and blue.
Map location: H – 18.
Maintenance: Clark Art Institute and Williams Outing Club.

For a slightly longer walk than the Pasture Loop, try a trip up to the Stone Bench. The bench is dedicated to George Moritz Wahl, a former professor of German at Williams College who climbed to this spot every evening to watch the sunset. During World War I he was subjected to substantial abuse because of his ethnic background, but when he died shortly after the war, his students and fellow townspeople erected the bench as a memorial and symbol of their regret. Although trees now obscure the view, the bench is a pleasant place for a quiet moment of reflection.

HOW TO GET THERE
• Refer to directions for the Pasture Loop.

DESCRIPTION
Begin at the trail sign and gravestones as for the **Pasture Loop.** At the first junction (0.3 mi.) continue straight to a gravel road that services Williamstown's buried water tank (0.4 mi.). The road links up to **Stone Hill Road** and the Stone Bench. For a more pleasant walk, cross the road and reenter the woods on a wide trail that ascends more steeply.

During fall and early winter a thick carpet of leaves covers the trail to make for a wonderful crinkle to your steps, but also slippery footing; beware. At 0.6 mi. the trail forks with a double orange blaze, straight ahead is the **Stone Hill Loop.** Bear right to find the stone bench. Over a small rise is the Stone Bench (0.7 mi.), a bit tilted after eighty years.

After a few minutes you can return by crossing a small clearing to the west and then following a path north to a gate. Alternatively, turn right (north) along Stone Hill Road to the gravel road and clearing. Ahead and to the left is another gate to enter the pasture. Either way, carefully close the gate behind you. Walk across the pasture to the grove of trees and follow the directions in the Pasture Loop section to return to the Clark Art Institute below (1.5 mi.).

STONE HILL LOOP

Distance: 2.3 miles.
Estimated time: 1.5 hours.
Blazes: Blue.
Map location: H - 18.
Maintenance: Williams Outing Club.

As its name suggests, this trail winds up and around Stone Hill, looping back to its starting point. It shares trails with the Pasture Loop and Stone Bench Loop. Take time to explore each of those as well and you have a nice morning or afternoon hike.

HOW TO GET THERE
• Refer to directions for the Pasture Loop.

DESCRIPTION
Start at the sign and gravestones, following the trail for the **Pasture Loop** through a variety of birch, beech and maple stands, as well as some hemlock and pine. Continue past the Pasture Loop turn-off to the right (0.3 mi.), across the gravel road (0.4 mi.) and uphill to a junction at 0.6 mi. (marked with a double orange blaze). One hundred yards to the right is the **Stone Bench**, while the Stone Hill Loop continues straight ahead.

Here is perhaps the most pleasant path on Stone Hill: wide, smooth, sinuous and rolling with hemlock groves and intermittent phyllite outcrops. In fall the bare trees afford a fantastic view east and south of the **Taconic Range**. At 0.9 mi. a lone hemlock marks a spot to sit, reflect and enjoy the view.

At a stone wall that once marked the boundary between two fields (1.0 mi.), a junction offers a spur trail directly to the **Gale Road Cut-off**. Bear left and follow a wide track down a couple switchbacks ignoring the logging roads that cross the trail. Small yellow diamonds on trees to the left mark Williamstown land and a hedgerow of large, old red oak and sugar maple dominate the boundary (1.7 mi.). At a small creek follow the sign straight-ahead across a footbridge, avoiding the roped off road to the right. The trail continues on town land to the gravel water tank road (2.0 mi.).

To return to the Clark Art Institute, turn right and descend to Gale Road. Proceed straight and enter the delivery or main entrance to the Clark on your left (2.3 mi.)

STONE HILL ROAD

Distance: 2.0 miles (approximately).
Estimated time: 50 minutes (one-way).
Blazes: None.
Map location: H - 18.
Maintenance: Williams Outing Club.

This, after all, was the prime North-South road in New England. Over this road went soldiers to Bennington in 1777; President Washington, riding over the hill in 1790, paused at this spot to take in what was then an open view of the fledgling town, with its new Free School; and every day townsfolk trafficked the road between North and South villages. To the struggling college this was the slender umbilicus of an indifferent world.

Arthur Latham Perry

HOW TO GET THERE
• Refer to directions for the Pasture Loop.

DESCRIPTION
From the Clark Art Institute, there are a number of ways to join Stone Hill Road. If on foot, you will enjoy the first 0.7 mi. of the

Stone Bench Loop described previously. Another option, described here, follows a wider road grade the entire way.

From the trailhead, return to South Street using the main or delivery entrance. Turn right and head towards the gated gravel road that ascends steeply as South Street becomes Gale Road and bears left. At the top of the steep rise, you see the **Stone Hill Loop** returning from the left; continue uphill. The Stone Bench loop crosses the road before you reach a field under which the Williamstown water tank lies buried.

Gravel gives way to mulch and dirt that lead to the Stone Bench on the left. If you have followed the Stone Bench Loop to this point, welcome. From here Stone Hill Road continues to the south, just below and to the west of the spine of Stone Hill. You will pass a number of quartzite outcrops on the left. At approximately 1.3 mi. the **Gale Road Cut-off** heads east while Stone Hill Road continues south. A number of fields border the road and offer fine views east and west.

At about 2.0 mi. Stone Hill Road becomes a maintained town road and continues to Scott Hill Road (2.6 mi.). From here you will want to return along the same route or be picked up; otherwise you face a long return trip on Route 7 or Route 43.

GALE ROAD CUT-OFF

Distances: 1.1 miles.
Estimated time: 40 minutes.
Blazes: Yellow (main trail) and yellow/blue (spur trail).
Map location: H – 16.
Maintenance: Williams Outing Club.

In 1994 the Williams Outing Club and townspeople cut this trail to connect Stone Hill Road to the Pine Cobble School, and Gale Road. A spur trail also connects it to the main Stone Hill Loop Trail.

HOW TO GET THERE
- Follow the description for Stone Hill Road. This trail begins on the east side of Stone Hill Road, 0.5 mi. beyond the Stone

Bench. A white sign stating "Trail East to Gale Road" marks the turn off.
- Alternatively, hike the Stone Hill Loop to the spur trail at 1.0 mi. and turn right (south). Walk 0.2 mi. to reach the yellow blazes of the Gale Road Cut-off.

DESCRIPTION

From **Stone Hill Road** (0.0 mi.), the trail ascends gently into the woods, passing through the remains of an old stone wall. After covering some rolling terrain, you reach the orange blazed spur trail that connects to the Stone Hill loop trail (0.1 mi.). From here, the Gale Road Cut-off makes a gradual descent through a mixed deciduous forest.

Just beyond a small clearing created by recent blow-down, watch for a sharp right turn down the hill, while an old wood road continues straight-ahead (0.3 mi.). Be aware of unstable footing and several crisscrossing skidder trails.

Cross a stream on a small log bridge (0.5 mi.) and ascend to a level open wood. Notice the old rusted gate left open one last time by a farmer years ago. Across another small stream the trail empties into a wide-open cornfield (0.7 mi.).

Atop the hill is a spectacular view of the **Greylock Range** to the southeast, **Pine Cobble** to the northeast and the **Dome** to the north. To reach Gale Road, follow the tree line left (north) to the foot of the hill (1.1 mi.). Please respect the lands of the Pine Cobble School. Turn left (northwest) on Gale Road to return to the Clark Art Institute.

GREEN MOUNTAIN

The Green Mountain Section includes the region north of the Hoosic River. Although several trails described lie in Vermont, they are described in this guide because the Dome and East Mountain effectively form a northern physiographic boundary of the North Berkshire area.

These mountains are the southern extremities of the Green Mountains, a range that extends several hundred miles north into Vermont. Although more than 400 million years old, the Green Mountains remain quite rugged, with sharp crests and steep slopes. The average elevation of the ridgeline today is 2,000 feet, with several peaks rising to heights of 4,000 feet or more. The lower slopes are covered with northern hardwoods, while above 3,000 feet are evergreen forests for which the range was named.

Recreational use of the Green Mountains began over 100 years ago with the construction of "summit houses", rustic hotels where vacationers could spend a few weeks enjoying the mountain scenery. The Green Mountain Club (GMC) was founded in 1910, and shortly afterward began construction of the Long Trail. This "footpath in the wilderness" now extends the length of Vermont, from the Massachusetts/Vermont line to the Canandian border, for a total of 265 miles. Pine Cobble trails serve as a southern gateway to the state border and Long Trail.

The GMC maintains over seventy primitive shelters and many tenting areas a moderate day's journey apart over the entire length of the trail. The southern 136 miles of the Long Trail also forms a link of the Appalachian Trail, a 2,150 mile (approximately) trail that extends the length of the Appalachian Mountains from Maine to Georgia.

PINE COBBLE TRAIL

Distances: 1.6 miles to Pine Cobble, 2.1 miles to Appalachian Trail.
Estimated time: 1 hour to Pine Cobble.
Blazes: Blue.
Map location: J – 19.
Maintenance: Williams Outing Club.

Pine Cobble (1,894 feet), to the northeast of Williamstown, offers one of the finest panoramic views of the Hoosic River valley. Within easy walking distance of the Williams College campus, this hike is a favorite with many Williams College students. The word "cobble" refers to the exposed outcropping of quartzite bedrock that is the destination of most of those who use the trail. On a clear day, the outcrop is easily visible from the valley floor, several miles away.

HOW TO GET THERE

If on foot, head north across the Williams campus. Pass the tennis courts and walk down Stetson Rd. to Cole Field. Follow the road around Eph's Pond, east through a gate to Cole Avenue. Turn left, cross the Hoosic River to the intersection with North Hoosac Rd. Diagonally right across North Hoosac Rd., Cole's Grove Rd., around a gate and into the Pine Cobble Development. At the mailboxes, turn right. The trailhead is 300 yards down the road on the left. By car:

- Take Route 2 east from its junction with Route 7.
- After 0.6 mi., turn left on Cole Ave. at the first stoplight.
- You will cross a bridge over the Hoosic River and railroad tracks just before North Hoosac Rd.
- Turn right on N. Hoosac (1.4 mi.) and then left on Pine Cobble Road at 1.8 miles.
- Park in the parking area on the left 0.2 mi. up the hill. The trailhead is across the road.

DESCRIPTION

At the Pine Cobble Trail sign (0.0 mi.) hike parallel to the road for 200 yards before turning left and ascending gradually into the woods. The trail levels out on a plateau (0.5 mi.), once the shore of glacial Lake Bascom that filled the entire Hoosac Valley to a depth of about 500 feet!

A side trail to the right marks the halfway point (0.8 mi.). It leads 350 feet downhill to Bear Spring, a slight upwelling at the base of a steep cliff topped with hemlocks. Since the spring is the only open water on the south side of Pine Cobble, it attracts many species of wildlife, including chipmunks, rabbits and deer.

Continue at a moderately steep grade, to a more level area at 1.0 mi. where the trail turns to the southeast. Yellow diamond-shaped tags mark the entrance to the WRLF Pine Cobble Summit Natural Area of Clarksburg State Forest. Cross two small jumbled rock outcroppings and follow a sharp left turn at the intersection with an old trail (1.1 mi.).

Watch for an unusual triplet oak tree with a water-filled basin at its center (1.4 mi.). After the original tree was cut down, three shoots sprouted around the edges of the old stump while the center rotted away. This flat section of the trail is also an excellent place to see trailing arbutus, the Massachusetts state flower, which usually blooms in early April.

A steep stretch completes the climb (1.5 mi.). From the trail sign at the crest of the hill, several short (0.1 mi.) trails to the right lead out onto the quartzite outcrops of Pine Cobble. Enjoy an excellent view of the **Greylock Range** across the valley to the south, with the summit of Mt. Greylock clearly distinguished by the war memorial and communications towers. The **Taconic Range** forms the western horizon, while the top of the **Dome** is visible to the north. Looking down into the **Hoosic River** valley, North Adams is to the east and Williamstown to the south.

From the trail sign north you pass an anchor point for an old fire tower and emerge onto a boulder field. A short climb leads to the summit of East Mountain, where the Pine Cobble Trail joins the **Appalachian Trail** (2.1 mi.). The site of an old forest fire, now covered with blueberry bushes, it provides nice views of the Taconic and Greylock Ranges.

PINE COBBLE VIA THE APPALACHIAN TRAIL

Distances: 2.5 miles to Pine Cobble Trail, 3.1 miles to Pine Cobble.
Estimated time: 1.5 hours.
Blazes: White.
Map location: M – 18.
Maintenance: Appalachian Mountain Club.

For an alternate route up Pine Cobble from the Hoosac Valley, try this portion of the Appalachian Trail (AT) along Sherman Brook. It is also the standard approach trail to the Long Trail of Vermont, which officially starts at the Massachusetts-Vermont border. In mid to late summer you may meet a "through-hiker" from Georgia following the Appalachian Trail to Mt. Katahdin in Maine.

HOW TO GET THERE
- Take Route 2 east from its junction with Route 7.
- After 0.6 mi., turn left on Cole Ave. at the first stoplight.
- You will cross a bridge over the Hoosic River and railroad tracks just before North Hoosac Rd.
- Turn right on N. Hoosac (1.4 mi.) and drive toward the historic Blackinton neighborhood (2.9 mi.). North Hoosac Rd. becomes Massachusetts Avenue in North Adams.
- You pass the AT Hoosic River footbridge to your right at 3.8 mi. note white blazes on the telephone poles.
- After 0.1 mi. (3.9 mi. total) the AT crosses Massachusetts Ave. at Sherman Brook and heads north.
- There is no parking at the trailhead, so arrange to be dropped off or park elsewhere. Protection Ave, 0.1 mi. east of Sherman Brook, is a good spot to pull off.

DESCRIPTION
From the stone bridge over Sherman Brook (0.0 mi.), follow a narrow lane north and cross two small footbridges before entering the woods (0.1 mi.). Follow the brook upstream for nearly a mile before making a short ascent out of the valley.

A blue-blazed side trail branches off to the left just beyond Pete's

Spring (1.4 mi.), and continues 0.1 mi. to a camping area, with three tent platforms, an outhouse, and a ready supply of water from both Pete's Spring and Sherman Brook.

Looping below the campsite, the AT passes a confluence of Sherman Brook and follows a tributary to the northwest (1.6 mi.). Note old bridge abutments from a former wood road crossing. At 2.2 mi. you pass the first junction with a Bad Weather Trail, which bypasses a difficult section of the main trail by looping to the southwest.

From here, the AT swings to the west, climbing a steep, rocky slope with good views to the south and east (2.3 mi.). White and flesh-colored quartzite talus covers the bottom of each steep slope. The Bad Weather Trail rejoins the main trail at the top of this section. A marshy area (2.4 mi.) and a rocky knoll complete the ascent at the Pine Cobble Trail intersection (2.5 mi.).

Here atop East Mountain are limited views of the Berkshire Hills to the south including the **Hoosac Range** (left), the **Taconic Range** (right) and the **Greylock Range** in between. From the junction, **Pine Cobble** is 0.7 mi. to the south (3.2 mi.). The **Appalachian Trail** continues to the right (north).

APPALACHIAN TRAIL
PINE COBBLE TRAIL TO COUNTY ROAD

Distances: 4.5 miles to County Road.
Estimated time: 2-3 hours.
Blazes: White.
Map location: L – 20.
Maintenance: Appalachian Mountain Club & Green Mtn. Club.

This attractive, well-traveled section of the Appalachian Trail (AT) traverses the ridge of East Mountain to the Vermont State Line. There begins the 265-mile Long Trail to Canada. North of the border is a campsite and shelter named for Seth Warner, patriot and Green Mountain Boy in the American Revolution. You may use the AT to connect the Broad Brook and Pine Cobble Trails for a pleasant, 10.2 mile hike.

HOW TO GET THERE
- Follow the Pine Cobble Trail 0.6 mi. past the summit of Pine Cobble or use the Appalachian Trail up Pine Cobble along Sherman Brook.

DESCRIPTION
From the **Pine Cobble Trail** and Appalachian Trail junction at East Mountain (0.0 mi.), proceed north across several quartzite outcrops. The largest of these exposed areas (0.5 mi.) is known as "Eph's Lookout" after Ephraim Williams, the founder of Williams College.

From here, the trail gradually descends the east side of the mountain, maintaining a fairly level grade except for a short rise just before the Massachusetts-Vermont State Line (1.4 mi.). Here a trail register marks the official southern end of the Long Trail (LT). The AT/LT descends sharply on log and stone steps through a mixed hemlock and deciduous forest, passing over two small brooks and looping east of a small ridge. Crossing the first of two dirt roads (3.1 mi.), the trail ascends steeply to the top of a small ridge, before descending into a marshy, fairly open area drained by two small streams (3.3 mi.).

Shortly after, you will intersect with West Road (4.0 mi.). To connect with the **Broad Brook Trail**, follow the road 0.3 mi. to the west and look for a sign to the left (southwest).

Just north of West Road, the AT/LT passes a side trail to the Seth Warner shelter (4.2 mi.). A short walk (0.2 mi.) west of the trail, the shelter has room for 6-8 people. A brook 350 feet west of the shelter provides water in spring, but is often dry during the summer months. A primitive camping area, with tent sites and a latrine, is located 0.2 mi. south on a spur trail.

Hike 0.3 mi. north of the Seth Warner spur trail on the AT/LT to reach County Road (4.5 mi.), a dirt road between the towns of Pownal and Stamford.

The AT/LT continues north 7.0 mi. to Congdon Camp and another 5.0 mi. to Route 9 in Vermont. For information on the Long Trail refer to the *Guide Book of the Long Trail* published by the **Green Mountain Club**.

BROAD BROOK TRAIL

Distances: 1.3 miles to Agawon Trail, 3.7 miles to County Road.
Estimated time: 2.5 hours.
Blazes: Blue.
Map location: J – 22.
Maintenance: Williams Outing Club.

This trail follows the course of Broad Brook as it winds around and up the eastern side of the Dome, passing through rugged and heavily wooded country. Since Broad Brook is the water supply for nearby towns, no swimming or camping is permitted in or along the brook.

HOW TO GET THERE
- Take Route 7 north towards Bennington.
- At 1.1 mi. you cross the Hoosic River flowing to the left (west).
- Turn right on Sand Springs Rd. at 1.6 miles. Keep right on main road until it becomes Bridges Road.
- Turn left on White Oaks Rd. (2.1 mi.) and drive uphill along Broad Brook.
- The pavement ends at the Vermont border (3.3 mi.). Cross Broad Brook. A pullout on the right marks the trailhead. Do not block the next driveway (gated) on the right.

DESCRIPTION
The trail begins at the northern corner of the parking lot (0.0 mi.). It briefly joins a dirt road, before bearing right into the woods (0.1 mi.), where it parallels a spillway of the North Adams waterworks. Stay on the right side of the stream, winding through a hemlock and spruce forest before crossing the brook for the first time (1.1 mi.). At high water these crossings may be treacherous or impossible. Use caution.

Just before a second crossing (1.3 mi.), a signpost marks the junction with the **Agawon Trail**, which diverges to the left and ascends to join the **Dome Trail**. From here, you follow the brook. Bear right and carefully cross the current on two large boulders.

Many of the boulders in Broad Brook are quartzite, a very hard rock that resists weathering and erosion.

A double blaze marks a fork (1.5 mi.) where a high-water trail climbs away to the right. The main trail continues straight ahead and crosses the brook twice before merging with the high-water trail on the right side of the brook. At 1.8 mi. an old wagon track connected to Henderson Road joins from the right (southeast), and both cross the brook. The road then climbs away to the left (northwest), as the trail resumes its old course along the brook.

Continue on the northwest bank of Broad Brook, cross a small tributary (2.3 mi.), and climb steeply through a dense pine forest. Descend back to the valley floor, cross another small stream (2.4 mi.), and ascend the shoulder on the northwest side of the brook, passing through a hemlock grove.

When you arrive at the convergence of two streams forming Broad Brook (3.0 mi.), the trail follows the tributary to the east. Cross the north branch, climb a hill between the two streams, turn right (3.1 mi.), and then descend to and cross the tributary again (3.3 mi.). The trail terminates at West Road after 3.7 miles.

To the left (north), West Road intersects **County Road**, which continues into Pownal, Vermont. To the right (southeast) you will cross the **Long Trail/Appalachian Trail** in 0.3 miles. The **Seth Warner Shelter** is a quarter mile north of West Road.

For a long loop, you may hike south to the Pine Cobble Trailhead using the Appalachian Trail and **Pine Cobble Trail** (5.3 mi.). The Broad Brook trailhead is 3.0 mi. by road from the Pine Cobble trailhead.

DOME TRAIL

Distances: 1.2 miles to Agawon Trail, 2.6 miles to summit.
Estimated time: 1.5 hours.
Blazes: Red.
Map location: J – 23.
Maintenance: Williams Outing Club.

Directly to the north of Williamstown, the Dome stands out among the surrounding mountains with its massive rounded summit. Although in Vermont, the Dome lures people from North Berkshire and forms a northern boundary of the area in this guide. The birch, maple, beech and oaks of the lower slopes transition to a distinctly Laurentian plateau (referring to the "Laurentide" ice of the last glacial period) with boreal forest near the summit. Red spruce and balsam fir characterize this vegetation zone, common in northern Canada, but found only on the Dome and Mt. Greylock in the North Berkshire area. The visual contrast created by these vegetation changes is easily visible from the Williamstown valley floor.

HOW TO GET THERE
- From Field Park, drive north on Route 7 toward Pownal.
- At 1.1 mi. you cross the Hoosic River flowing to the left (west).
- Turn right on Sand Springs Rd. at 1.6 miles. Keep right on main road until it becomes Bridges Road.
- Turn left on White Oaks Rd. (2.1 mi.) and drive uphill along Broad Brook.
- The pavement ends at the Vermont border (3.3 mi.), follow the dirt road farther uphill past a small pond to a pullout on the right (3.6 mi.). There is a sign and chained road.

DESCRIPTION
From White Oaks Road (0.0 mi.), follow an old wood road through a clearing and enter the forest heading east (0.2 mi.). The trail ascends steadily and at 0.5 mi. takes a sharp left (northwest) off the wood road (follow blazes). You pass through several Y inter-sections with logging roads and paths (follow blazes). Since ero-sion has stripped much of the soil in this section, watch your foot-ing. Follow reroutes and try to avoid widening the trail.

At 1.2 mi. you reach a junction with the **Agawon Trail** (yellow blazes), which bears off to the right. Just beyond is Meeting House Rock (1.3 mi.), a large white rock that roughly marks halfway to the summit.

Continue past the rock to an intersection marked by an aban-doned truck (1.7 mi.). Bear right (northeast) and follow the marked trail over a series of small terraces and through several jogs left and right. Near the summit you emerge onto a ledge, dip down into a boggy area, and ascend to a last series of ledges that extend to the top of the mountain (2.6 mi.).

From the 2,748-foot summit you have a view somewhat screened by trees, but still magnificent, of the entire North Berkshire area. Unfold your map and pick out **Pine Cobble**, the **Greylock Range** and the **Taconic Range**.

Between the spruce bog and the summit, blackberry and hobblebush border the trail to welcome weary hikers in the fall. The flat top of the Dome is also attractive in winter when snow and frost cover every needle of the spruce and balsam fir.

AGAWON TRAIL

Distance: 0.7 miles, Dome Trail to Broad Brook Trail.
Estimated time: 20–30 minutes.
Blazes: Yellow.
Map location: K - 24.
Maintenance: Williams Outing Club.

Williams College students cleared the Agawon Trail in the spring of 1959, to provide a route from Dome Trail to Broad Brook with a minimum of new trail mileage. Together the Dome, Agawon and Broad Brook Trails form a pleasant 6.5 mi. circuit.

HOW TO GET THERE

- From the Dome Trail: Follow the Dome Trail for 1.2 mi. from its trailhead. The junction with the Agawon Trail, clearly marked with a trail sign, is on the right just below Meeting House Rock, an obvious large boulder.
- From the Broad Brook Trail: After the second stream crossing from the White Oaks Road trailhead (1.3 mi.), a sign marks the Agawon trail junction to the left (northwest).

DESCRIPTION

From the Dome Trail, the Agawon Trail heads off to the northeast. After about 100 yards, follow a sharp right turn and descend. A small brook appears on the left before disappearing underground. The trail becomes steeper, eventually emerging onto a bluff overlooking Broad Brook. There it turns right and intersects with the Broad Brook trail after a last 100 yards.

TACONIC RANGE

The Taconic Mountain Range forms the western edge of North Berkshire, a north to south line shared with the Massachusetts-New York boundary. A series of regularly spaced stream valleys, referred to as "Hollows", cut and drain each side of the range. During the 18th and 19th centuries, much of the forests were cleared to the Taconic Crest and nearly every hollow had a road climbing from Williamstown, up and over to New York. Today forests have reclaimed farmland, Route 2 is the main east-west road over the range and many abandoned roads serve as the trails described in this section.

Like the Green Mountains, most of the Taconic Range is forested with northern hardwoods, but open meadows in some high areas offer excellent views of the surrounding mountains. From Berlin Mountain (2,798 feet), it is possible to see not only the Berkshires and the Green Mountains, but also the mountains along the Hudson–the Catskills, Helderbergs and Adirondacks.

The principal trail in the Taconic Section is the Taconic Crest Trail, which runs 35 miles from Petersburg, New York to Route 20 in Pittsfield, Massachusetts. In the last decade, three states and several non-profit groups have successfully purchased much of the ridge from private owners, but hikers should be aware that a few sections of the trail still cross private land. Please respect posted property in those areas.

Feeder trails from Williamstown to the Taconic Crest Trail include the Birch Brook Trail, R.R.R. Brooks Trail, Berlin Pass Trail, Class of '33 Trail, Phelps Trail, Mills Hollow Trail and Bentley Hollow Trail. Full information concerning the entire Taconic Crest Trail can be obtained from either the Taconic Hiking Club or the Williamstown Rural Lands Foundation.

HOPKINS FOREST LOOP TRAIL

Distances: 1.5 miles Lower Loop, 2.6 miles Upper Loop.
Estimated time: 2 hours (both loops).
Map location: H – 20.
Blazes: None.
Maintenance: Williams College Center for Environmental Studies.

Hopkins Memorial Forest is a 2,425-acre research site operated by the Williams College Center for Environmental Studies (CES). There are a wide variety of forest types, ranging from recently overgrown farmland to old woodlot stands of the 19th century. Old farm roads, stone walls and partially visible cellar holes reflect the complex human history of the property.

Much of this information is recorded in *Farms to Forest*, a naturalist's guide published by the Center for Environmental Studies and available in local bookstores. This book also features a "guided" tour of the ecology of the lower loop trail. Research projects are in progress throughout the forest. To avoid disturbing them, please stay on trails and do not remove stakes or other markers.

The Hopkins Memorial Forest Loop Trail is actually a figure eight composed of a 1.5 mi. lower loop and 2.6 mi. upper loop. Information at the Rosenburg Center describes more trails within the forest.

HOW TO GET THERE
- From Field Park take Route 7 north to Bulkley Street (0.3 mi.)
- Turn left on Bulkley Street, cross a bridge over Hemlock Brook (0.4 mi.) and ascend a long gradual rise.
- When you reach the T-junction with Northwest Hill Road (1.1 mi.), turn right.
- The entrance to Hopkins Memorial Forest is on your left. Please park in the first parking area to the left.
- A few hundred feet beyond is the Rosenburg Center, which contains a small historical museum; and the Moon Barn, a historic structure that once stood on the farm in the center of Hopkins Memorial Forest belonging to Alfred C. Moon.

DESCRIPTION

The Lower Loop starts at the Moon Barn (0.0 mi.) along a carriage road improved by the Civilian Conservation Corps during the 1930s. Walk to the right past the Outing Club Cabin (0.1 mi.) and an experimental weather station in a vestigial field. The trail winds through forest of various composition and age (refer to *Farms to Forest* for more natural history) before reaching a four-way intersection (0.8 mi.).

To return to the Moon Barn via the Lower Loop, turn left, away from the Upper Loop. This section of the trail may be a little swampy in the spring, but please resist the temptation to trample the vegetation to either side. After a level section the trail descends steeply back to the Rosenburg center. (1.5 mi.)

For a longer hike, venture on to the Upper Loop Trail (2.6 mi.). If in search of the **Birch Brook Trail**, follow the north (right) leg of the loop for a more direct approach. Otherwise, choose either at your whim. The wide path was once a carriage road from which Amos Lawrence Hopkins would view his estate.

The trail crosses the middle and north branches of Birch Brook while passing through beautiful forest. This route is a fantastic ski or snowshoe jaunt with enough snow, but take it in the clockwise direction. Upon return to the four-way intersection, return along the Lower Loop for a 4.1 mi. total trip.

BIRCH BROOK TRAIL

Distance: 1.4 miles.
Estimated time: 1 hour.
Map location: E – 21.
Blazes: Blue.
Maintenance: Williams Outing Club.

This spur trail to the Taconic Crest Trail takes you through the Hopkins Memorial Forest from the Loop Trail. The trail begins at the north branch of Birch Brook, its namesake.

HOW TO GET THERE
• Follow directions to the Hopkins Forest Loop Trail.

• Hike the lower loop to the four-way intersection (1.0 mi.), turn right, and proceed to the Birch Brook Trail (1.7 mi.).

DESCRIPTION

From the trail entrance (0.0 mi.), the trail heads west, briefly paralleling the North Branch of Birch Brook before jogging north, away from the stream. You hike mostly on old road grades with intermittent reroutes to avoid heavily eroded sections.

There are several beautiful patches of ferns along the trail as you climb toward the Taconic Crest. The forest in this area is susceptible to blow down during storms. If trees block the trail, try to go over, rather than around, and please report trail conditions to the Williams Outing Club.

Shortly after the Massachusetts-New York border, the Birch Brook Trail terminates at a signpost marking the junction with the **Taconic Crest Trail** at 1.5 miles.

The Snow Hole is 1.6 mi. north and North Pownal is 4.5 mi. farther. To the south are the **Shepherd's Well Trail** (0.6 mi.) and Route 2 (1.1 mi.).

FITCH TRAIL

Distances: 0.7 mile to Bee Hill, 1.1 miles to R.R.R. Brooks Trail.
Estimated time: 30 minutes to Bee Hill.
Blazes: Blue diamonds.
Map location: G – 18.
Maintenance: Williamstown Rural Lands Foundation.

For a short hike you can ascend Bee Hill through the Edward H. Fitch Memorial Woodlands protected by the Williamstown Rural Lands Foundation. For a pleasant loop, link up with the R.R.R. Brooks Trail and return to your car along Bee Hill Road.

HOW TO GET THERE

• From the intersection of Routes 2 and 7, take Route 7 south.
• Turn right on Bee Hill Road (0.6 mi.), drive up the hill, over a bridge (0.8 mi.) and up a steep hill.

• At 1.3 mi. a wooden sign on the right marks the Fitch Trail. Several small pullouts along the left side of the road provide space for 2-3 cars. Within 0.1 mi. are three more, larger pullouts for additional parking.

DESCRIPTION

From Bee Hill Road (0.0 mi.), follow the well-marked path on gentle grades through young forest. At 0.7 mi. you reach the rounded top of Bee Hill where only a few decades ago you would have had a clear view of the **Greylock Range** and valley below.

For a 2.4 mi. loop, continue over the west side of the hill to meet up with the **R.R.R. Brooks Trail** (1.1 mi.) near an old Boy Scout shelter. Turn right to reach Bee Hill Rd. (1.9 mi.) through Flora Glen. To return to your car, turn right and walk 0.5 mi. uphill to the Fitch Trail parking.

R.R.R. BROOKS TRAIL

Distances: 1.8 miles to Old Petersburg Road, 2.4 miles to Shepherd's Well Trail, 2.9 miles to Route 2.
Estimated time: 2.0 hours.
Map location: G – 18.
Blazes: Blue.
Maintenance: Williams Outing Club.

Running parallel to Route 2, this trail offers hikers a direct route from Williamstown to Petersburg Pass, passing through the 930-acre Taconic Trail State Park along the way. It is named for a former dean of Williams College, who lived on Bee Hill Road and originally cleared the trail. One of the highlights is Flora Glen, a beautiful wooded area that is believed to have been the inspiration for William Cullen Bryant's poem *Thanatopsis*.

HOW TO GET THERE

• From the intersection of Routes 2 and 7, take Route 7 south.
• Turn right on Bee Hill Road (0.6 mi.) and drive up the hill and over a bridge. A sign marks the trailhead.

• As of 1998, residential construction eliminated parking at the historic trailhead. Please do not park on private land. Instead, continue along Bee Hill Road to the Fitch Trail (1.3 mi.). Several small pullouts along the left side of the road provide space for 2-3 cars here. Within 0.1 mi. are three more, larger pullouts for additional parking.

DESCRIPTION

Although the **Fitch Trail** provides access to the R.R.R. Brooks Trail and makes a nice 1.8 mi. loop, this description will assume you have walked 0.5 mi. down Bee Hill Rd. to the trailhead, or been dropped off.

The trail begins at the south end of a defunct dam (0.0 mi.) and skirts a former pond, drained in 1997. This section borders private property, so please be respectful and walk only on the trail. Here is Flora Glen, nearly always wet, and a sea of ferns during the spring and summer months.

Vegetation alternates between northern hardwood (mostly maple, beech and birch) and evergreen (spruce and hemlock) as you walk along the valley side above the stream. The trail descends to the level of the stream (0.5 mi.), and makes an abrupt left (0.6 mi.) to climb steeply up a series of steps out of the streambed. Just below the remains of an old Boy Scout shelter (0.8 mi.), the Fitch Trail enters from the left.

After a bridge (0.9 mi.), you pass through a forest of birch and beech trees, and emerge at the edge of a large field (1.4 mi.). A sign identifies the R.R.R Brooks Trail for descending hikers.

Hike uphill (west) through the field and stay left (south) of the tree island. Tall grass can make for difficult navigation across this open area. Your path and Route 2 will gradually converge towards the Old Petersburg Rd (1.8 mi.). If you are misplaced when you hit this double track jeep road, walk toward Route 2 (south) to pick up the upper section of R.R.R Brooks.

Across Route 2 from Old Petersburg Road is a pull-out where a vehicle shuttle could be arranged. To continue toward the Taconic Crest, enter the woods 250 feet from Route 2 on a wide path marked by a sign and blue blazes. You merge with a road grade from the left and parallel Route 2 up a gentle ascent on this wide-open trail.

At 2.4 mi. you will reach the junction with the **Shepherd's Well Trail**. To the left, the R.R.R Brooks Trail continues on a dirt road, until it makes a short descent to the left that leads to Route 2 (2.9 mi.). There is no parking at Route 2. The Petersburg Pass Scenic area is 0.4 mi. west along the road.

SHEPHERD'S WELL TRAIL

Distance: 1.0 mile to Taconic Crest Trail.
Estimated time: 40 minutes.
Map location: D – 19.
Blazes: Blue.
Maintenance: Williams Outing Club.

HOW TO GET THERE
• Via the R.R.R. Brooks Trail or the Taconic Crest Trail.

DESCRIPTION
From the **R.R.R. Brooks Trail** junction (0.0 mi.), the Shepherd's Well Trail branches to the right and climbs gently through a forest of maple, beech and oak trees.

A white sign indicates the boundary of **Hopkins Memorial Forest** (0.4 mi.). As you enter the forest, notice the red and yellow bands painted on the trees. These are part of a permanent grid system for vegetation surveys, established by the United States Forest Service in 1936 and still maintained by Williams College professors and students.

Just beyond a double blaze signaling an abrupt left turn, the trail enters an open area filled with huckleberries and blueberries. The spectacular view encompasses the **Greylock Range** to the east and the **Taconic Range**, the **Old Williams Ski Area** and **Petersburg Pass** to the south.

Across the clearing, the trail levels off, descends gradually and turns right (0.9 mi.) to skirt the ridge. To the right was once a well belonging to a farmer named Shepherd, but all traces of it have now disappeared.

Follow the contour around the rise in the ridge to meet the **Taconic Crest Trail** at a trail sign (1.0 mi.).

WRLF LOOP TRAIL

Distance: 1.4 miles.
Estimated time: 1 hour.
Blazes: Blue diamond markers.
Map location: C – 17.
Maintenance: Williamstown Rural Lands Foundation.

During the summer of 1998, the Williamstown Rural Lands Foundation designed and installed this short interpretive loop trail. Small signs along the trail offer natural history information to hikers.

HOW TO GET THERE
• Refer to directions for the Class of '33 Trail.

DESCRIPTION
From the parking area you may start directly on the Haley Brook Cut-off Trail for a shorter loop or walk 400 feet back down the road you drove in on to the Loop Trail and Class of '33 Trail trailhead.

Each trail is well blazed to and across Haley Brook to a relatively level logging grade south of the brook. On the road, walk west. To the left (south) you will pass four old pits used to make charcoal from trees on this land. The trail ends at the **Old Williams College Ski Area** from whence you may retrace your steps or return via Berlin Road.

CLASS OF '33 OR BERLIN MOUNTAIN TRAIL

Distances: 2.0 miles.
Estimated time: 1.5 hours.
Blazes: Blue.
Map location: C – 17.
Maintenance: Williams Outing Club.

Members of the Williams Outing Club constructed this trail up Berlin Mountain in the fall of 1933. Slightly longer than the route via the Berlin Pass Trail, it is an extremely pretty hike through classic New England mountain woods.

HOW TO GET THERE

- Take Routes 7 and 2 southwest to where they split (2.3 mi.).
- Turn right (west) on Route 2 and then left on Torrey Woods Road (2.6 mi.).
- At the first intersection, continue straight (3.0 mi.).
- At a fork (3.8 mi.) follow the left road (Berlin Mountain Road) uphill and past a number of houses to the trailhead, clearly signed on the left.
- There is room to park 2-3 cars about 400 feet beyond on the left (4.7 mi.).

DESCRIPTION

From the parking area is a cut-off for the **Williamstown Rural Lands Foundation** (WRLF) **Loop Trail**. To access the Class of '33 trail or the entire Loop Trail, walk 400 feet back the way you drove in. On the south side is a signed trailhead (0.0 mi.) and a trail blazed with blue paint swatches (WOC) as well as blue diamond markers (WRLF).

Follow blazes through left and right turns to Haley Brook and the first interpretive sign of the WRLF Loop Trail (0.2 mi.). Cross the brook and climb the far bank to a well-signed junction. Bear left (east) to stay on the Class of '33 Trail, where the Loop Trail continues to the right. Follow blazes uphill and right (south) through hemlocks and up a deeply gullied logging grade (0.4 mi.) to a level area and hemlock grove.

Descend to the site of the old Williams Outing Club Berlin Cabin marked by remains of an outhouse (0.7 mi.). Heed a sharp right switchback to the brook then gain a logging grade on the far side. Bear left to follow a steady steep grade to the mountain ridge above. At 1.2 mi. you will gain the ridge leading west to the summit of Berlin Mountain.

Logging in the years 1995-1997 widened old wood roads in a confusing network. Large blue blazes mark a boundary line, not the trail that follows the ridgeline logging road. If you start to head downhill, you are going the wrong way. Stay high on the ridge. At 1.5 mi. is a fantastic view of **Broad Brook** and the **Dome** to the northeast.

At 1.8 mi. continue straight on the ridge through a confusing nexus of roads towards the summit. One last turn left up the top of the **Old Williams College Ski Area** will bring you to the clear summit of Berlin Mountain (2.0 mi.).

Four small cement piers mark the site of an old fire tower. A panoramic view northeast to southeast includes all the areas described in this guide. To the southwest are the rolling hills of Southeast Hollow, with the Catskills rising in the distance. Albany and Troy are visible to the west and on a clear day you might see the southern Adirondacks to the northwest.

There are three options for return to the parking lot. You may retrace your route on the Class of '33 Trail for a 4.0 mi. round trip. Alternatively, instead of taking your first right onto the '33 Trail, continue straight (northeast) down the abandoned ski slope (3.5 mi. total). This route is unmaintained and extremely steep. Use caution.

Finally, you may follow the **Taconic Crest Trail** (white markers) and off-road vehicle tracks north to the **Berlin Pass Trail** and back to your vehicle (4.3 mi.).

BERLIN PASS TRAIL

Distances: 0.8 mile to Berlin Pass, 2.0 miles to Berlin Mountain.
Estimated time: 45 minutes to Berlin Pass.
Blazes: Blue.
Map location: C – 18.
Maintenance: Williams Outing Club.

For an afternoon hike or direct access to the Taconic Crest Trail, try the Berlin Pass Trail. It was once a section of the Boston-Albany post road, one of two dozen such roads through the Berkshires that were used to deliver everything from newspapers to packages. A one mile walk leads to wind-swept meadows with panoramic views almost equivalent to those of the Class of '33 Trail.

HOW TO GET THERE
- Take Routes 7 and 2 southwest to where they split (2.3 mi.).
- Turn right (west) on Route 2 and then left on Torrey Woods Road (2.6 mi.).
- At the first intersection, continue straight (3.0 mi.).
- At a fork (3.8 mi.) follow the left road (Berlin Mountain Road).
- Continue straight to a dead end below the Old Williams College Ski Area (5.1 mi.).
- Park on the right side of the ski area parking lot.

DESCRIPTION
From the ski area parking lot (0.0 mi.), follow a jeep road into the woods on the north (right when driving in) side. The trail swings west through a mixed hardwood forest of ash, sugar maple, poplar and red oak. Just off to the right is a gray stone pillar marking the boundary between Massachusetts and New York.

As the trail continues to climb, soil grows rockier and the composition of the forest begins to change; beech and paper birch mix with oak, hop hornbeam and red maple. After crossing a brook, the trail emerges into the brushy saddle known as Berlin Pass.

At Berlin Pass, the old stage route crosses the **Taconic Crest Trail** (TCT) before descending the western slope of the Taconic Range to Berlin, New York. If you continue on the TCT, which runs north-south across the pass, **Berlin Mountain** is 1.2 mi. south and **Petersburg Pass** is 1.5 mi. to the north.

For a loop back to the parking lot you may climb Berlin Mountain and then descend via the steep and unmaintained **Old Williams College Ski Area** (3.0 mi.) or the **Class of '33 Trail** (4.5 mi.).

OLD WILLIAMS COLLEGE SKI AREA

Distance: 1.0 mile.
Estimated time: 45 minutes.
Blazes: None.
Map location: B – 18.
Maintenance: None.

Williams College cut this extremely steep ski trail in the old New England tradition: steep, narrow and winding. NCAA Division I skiers from across New England raced this course in the 1960s and 1970s. Today most use this trail as a descent route to complete a loop with the Class of '33 Trail or Berlin Pass Trail.

HOW TO GET THERE
- Take Routes 7 and 2 south to where they diverge (2.3 mi.).
- Turn right (west) on Route 2 and then left on Torrey Woods Road (2.6 mi.).
- At the first intersection, continue straight (3.0 mi.).
- At a fork (3.8 mi.) follow the left-hand road (Berlin Mountain Road) uphill and past a number of houses.
- Continue straight to a dead end below the Old Williams College Ski Area (5.1 mi.).

DESCRIPTION
Most people use this route for a descent; but if you want a punishing uphill grunt, this is the trail for you. To find the trail coming down from Berlin Mountain, refer to the **Class of '33 Trail** description. An obvious clear area heads directly up the steep north side of Berlin Mountain, south of the parking area (0.0 mi.). Dirt bikes have created a number of user trails up the slope, choose your course.

Above the ski slope narrows and winds through a series of turns. Look down and imagine racing around these bends on skis! Near the summit of Berlin Mountain, the Class of '33 Trail merges from the left (0.9 mi.). A short walk further takes you to the summit, a fantastic view at the site of an old fire tower and the **Taconic Crest Trail**.

FIELD FARM

Distance: 4.5 miles of trails.
Estimated time: Your choice.
Blazes: Yellow.
Map location: D – 13.
Maintenance: The Trustees of Reservations.

The Trustees of Reservations manage this 296-acre property that has been farmed continuously since the founding of Williamstown. A 4.5 mi. system of loop trails visits the varied habitats on this terrace that formed in glacial Lake Bascom about 14,500 years ago. A suggested donation of $2.00 helps maintain the trails.

HOW TO GET THERE
- Take Route 7 south from Williamstown to Five Corners (4.1 mi.), the junction with Route 43 (flashing light).
- Turn right on Route 43, and immediately right on Sloan Road (west).
- One mile up Sloan Road is the signed entrance to Field Farm (5.1 mi. on the right).
- Enter the property and take the first right to an information board and parking area.

DESCRIPTION
At the trailhead are maps to the 4.5 mi. network of trails. Choose from South Trail, Pond Trail, North Trail or the Oak Loop for hiking, fishing, nature study, cross country skiing, picnicking or photography. Yellow blazes and green and white directional signs guide the way. Trails are open during daylight hours.

PHELPS TRAIL

Distance: 1.9 miles to the Taconic Crest Trail.
Estimated time: 1 hour.
Map location: C – 13.
Blazes: Blue.
Maintenance: Williamstown Rural Lands Foundation.

This trail, constructed in the 1990s, ascends a ridge jutting out east from the Taconic Range, providing access to the Taconic Crest Trail.

HOW TO GET THERE

- Take Route 7 south from Williamstown to Five Corners (4.1 mi.), the junction with Route 43 (flashing light).
- Turn right on Route 43, and immediately right on Sloan Road (west).
- Go west on Sloan Road to the T-intersection with Oblong Road, and turn left (5.3 mi.).
- The trailhead is on the right (west), at a parking area marked with blue State Forest boundary tags and a large sign (5.6 mi.).

DESCRIPTION

From the trail sign (0.0 mi.), follow blue blazes west across an open field and into the woods. After crossing a fence line, enter an area of fir and hemlock trees before the intersection with an old wood road (0.2 mi.).

Turn left onto the wood road and climb moderately into a mixed deciduous forest where the trail turns sharply to the right in the first of several switchbacks (0.3 mi.). The trail turns sharply right to leave a wood road and climb more steeply at 0.7 miles.

At 1.0 mi., the trail crosses through a gap in the first of three old stone walls. Shortly after crossing the second stone wall, the trail rounds the shoulder of the spur, coming close to the State Forest boundary, where it turns to the right and continues upwards. (Be careful not to confuse the blazes marking the trail with the large blue paint swatches that indicate the boundary line). After crossing the third stone wall (1.3 mi.), you crest the spur, leveling out briefly before beginning the final ascent to the **Taconic Crest Trail** (1.9 mi.).

The Taconic Crest Trail (TCT) runs north to south along the range crest. It is blazed with white diamond tags nailed to trees along the trail. Some tags have been painted day-glow orange by snowmobile and all-terrain vehicle users. From the Phelps Trail/ TCT junction, **Berlin Mountain** is approximately 1.9 mi. to the north. 1.0 mi. to the south is the junction of the TCT, **Mills Hollow** and Southeast Hollow Trails.

MILLS HOLLOW TRAIL

Distance: 1.6 miles.
Estimated time: 1 hour.
Blazes: Blue diamonds.
Map location: C – 12.
Maintenance: Town of Williamstown.

Mills Hollow was once the only route from South Williamstown over the Taconic Range to Albany and other New York towns. Recent efforts secured an easement to protect access for this byway to the Taconic Crest Trail.

HOW TO GET THERE
- Take Route 7 south from Williamstown to Five Corners (4.1 mi.), the junction with Route 43 (flashing light).
- Turn right on Route 43, and immediately right on Sloan Road (west).
- Go west on Sloan Road to the T-intersection with Oblong Road, and turn left (5.3 mi.).
- Park at the Phelps Trail trailhead on the right (west), marked with blue State Forest boundary tags and a large sign (5.6 mi.).
- The Mills Hollow Trail starts 0.4 mi. farther along Oblong Rd (6.0 mi. total). Use the gravel road past a red gate.

DESCRIPTION

From Oblong Road the Mills Hollow Trail (0.0 mi.) begins on a gravel road a couple hundred feet south of a red gate. The gate marks the historic Mills Hollow access, now closed by a new easement agreement.

Follow the gravel road across a field and into the woods; please respect the private property in this area. The road grade climbs steadily up the north side of Mills Hollow.

At 1.6 mi. you reach the **Taconic Crest Trail** (TCT) at the Massachusetts and New York state boundary. Southeast Hollow drops west into New York. A nice loop may be made with the **Phelps Trail** (4.7 mi. total) in either direction.

BENTLY HOLLOW TRAIL

Distance: 1.2 miles.
Estimated time: 45 minutes.
Blazes: Blue diamonds.
Map location: B – 9.
Maintenance: Taconic Hiking Club.

Bently Hollow is a historic route over the Taconic Range to Mattison Hollow and Cherry Plain, New York. This steep climb has areas of robust spring ephemeral wildflowers.

HOW TO GET THERE

- Take Route 7 south from Williamstown to Five Corners (4.1 mi.), the junction with Route 43 (flashing light).
- Turn right on Route 43 and drive south.
- At the Williamstown/Hancock line (7.0 mi.) be ready for a turnoff.
- 0.6 mi. beyond the town line, turn right atop a rise into what looks like a driveway. A metal gate across Route 43 marks the turn. Drive a couple hundred yards west; a sign points "To Taconic Crest Trail".
- Park off the road; do not block the private driveways in this area.

DESCRIPTION

Walk directly west and uphill to gain the historic road grade now rutted and eroded. Scattered blue diamonds mark the route as you climb up the north side of Bently Hollow on a steep grade to the **Taconic Crest Trail**. During the spring, take time to enjoy a profusion of wildflowers in spots along the way.

At the Taconic Crest you may hike north or south, but plan a car shuttle at other trailheads. For years the Mattison Hollow Trail to the west has been closed to public access. Recent efforts of the Trust for Public Land and the New York State Department of Environmental Conservation will reopen the trail for the new millennium. Please heed postings as access changes.

TACONIC CREST TRAIL

The Taconic Crest Trail runs 35 miles along the Taconic Range from Pittsfield, Massachusetts to Petersburg, New York at an average elevation at 2,200 feet. Hikers, mountain bikers, skiers, snowmobilers and off-road vehicle users share what has become a wide, braided trail system.

White, diamond-shaped markers along the length of the trail mark the route, although some have been spray-painted orange. Feeder trails from the east and west generally have blue diamond markers or blue painted blazes.

Access from North Berkshire includes, from north to south: Birch Brook Trail, R.R.R. Brooks and Shepherd's Well Trails, Petersburg Pass, Berlin Pass Trail, Class of '33 Trail, Phelps Trail, Mills Hollow Trail and Bently Hollow Trail. All are described in the Taconic Range section of this guide.

During late summer, water may be difficult to find near the crest. Plan accordingly; carry extra water and be prepared for long sidehikes to fill up your water bottles.

Many organizations combine efforts to manage and protect the Taconic Trail system that also includes the South Taconic Trail. Thanks to the Taconic Hiking Club, Appalachian Mountain Club, Williamstown Rural Lands Foundation and the National Park Service.

TACONIC CREST TRAIL
NORTH OF PETERSBURG PASS

Distances: 0.4 mile to Shepherd's Well Trail, 1.0 mile to Birch
    Brook Trail, 2.6 miles to Snow Hole.
Estimated time: 1.5 hours to Snow Hole.
Blazes: White diamonds.
Map location: B – 20.
Maintenance: Taconic Hiking Club.

From Petersburg Pass Scenic Area a short hike accesses beautiful
views along White Rocks and the spur trails of Shepherd's Well
and Birch Brook. Farther north, the Snow Hole often holds snow
and ice well into summer.

HOW TO GET THERE
- Take Routes 7 and 2 southwest to where they split (2.3 mi.).
- Follow Route 2 west to Petersburg Pass (6.2 mi.).
- Park on the left (south) side of Route 2 at Petersburg Pass
  Scenic Area.

DESCRIPTION
Walk north across the highway (0.0 mi.) and up a steep bank to an
open shrubby area with fine views. The trail stays west of the
ridgeline until you pass the **Shepherd's Well** trail on the right at
0.4 mile. Continue north into a large clearing with panoramic views,
particularly from the knoll. This first mile of trail is known as
White Rocks, named after the outcroppings of white quartz vein.

At 1.0 mi. the **Birch Brook Trail** leads east to the **Hopkins
Memorial Forest Loop Trail**. Farther north, you enter Vermont
and then return to New York following the ridge. At 2.6 mi. a
short path forking to the right leads to the Snow Hole, a deep
bedrock cleft that holds snow and ice well into summer and
occasionally the year round.

Another 4.5 mi. north the Taconic Crest Trail ends at Prosser Hollow Road, off Route 22 in Petersburg, New York. As of summer 1999, a new trailhead provided by the New York Department of Environmental Conservation and the Taconic Hiking Club will allow the trail to continue to Route 346.

TACONIC CREST TRAIL
SOUTH OF PETERSBURG PASS

Distances: 1.5 miles to Berlin Pass Trail, 2.7 miles to Berlin Mountain, 5.2 to Mills Hollow, 8.2 miles to Bently Hollow.
Estimated time: 1.5 hours to Berlin Mountain.
Blazes: White diamonds.
Map location: B – 20.
Maintenance: Taconic Hiking Club.

Petersburg Pass Scenic Area provides a convenient access to the Taconic Crest Trail and spur trails to the south. The views from Berlin Mountain may be attained with a couple hour hike. Motorized vehicles have created a network of trails along the ridge. Try to follow blazes, and stay high on the crest.

HOW TO GET THERE
- Take Routes 7 and 2 southwest to where they split (2.3 mi.).
- Follow Route 2 west up the Taconic Range to Petersburg Pass (6.2 mi.).
- Park on the left (south) side of Route 2 at Petersburg Pass Scenic Area.

DESCRIPTION
Start right (west) of the ridge (0.0 mi.) and ascend the wood road toward the crest. You will skirt west of Mt. Raimer, where a ski lift once served a small system of trails now growing over.

You pass through an open area (1.0 mi.) then descend to Berlin Pass (1.5 mi.) where the **Berlin Pass Trail** joins from the left. Continue south through alternating woods and meadow. At 2.0

mi. an abandoned charcoal furnace lies fifty yards west of the trail. The summit of **Berlin Mountain** affords a 360 degree view (2.7 mi.).

The Taconic Crest Trail continues southeast through a spruce grove and then a short hardwood forest. From a saddle at 4.7 mi. you may find water at a small spring about 300 feet to the west.

At 5.2 mi. you reach a saddle and the **Mills Hollow Trail** near the New York–Massachusetts boundary. Water may be found about 0.7 mi. to the west into Southeast Hollow.

Another 3.0 mi. south through forest and field and over several knobs leads to a saddle and the **Bently Hollow Trail**.

The Taconic Crest Trail continues 19.4 mi. south to Route 20 past Rathburn Hollow, Rounds Mountain, the Town of Hancock, Poppy Mountain, and Berry Pond. For more information refer to the *AMC Massachusetts and Rhode Island Trail Guide*.

GREYLOCK RANGE

Mt. Greylock rises over 2,500 feet above the Green and Hoosic River valleys in North Berkshire County. For centuries Greylock has drawn people for hunting, gathering, farming, grazing, timber, scientific observations and recreation. Some say that the mountain was named for a local Indian chief, who was nicknamed "Gray Lock", while others contend that its name refers to the clouds that frequently sheath the summit.

The highest point in the state of Massachusetts, Mt. Greylock offers one of the most spectacular 360-degree panoramas available. A granite tower at the summit was built as a war memorial for the citizens of Massachusetts. From the observation platform at the top of the 92-foot tower you may see between 70 and 100 miles. On a clear day, it is possible to identify landmarks in four different states including: Vermont's Green Mountains to the north, New Hampshire's Mt. Monadnock to the northeast, and Pontoosuc and Onota Lakes in Pittsfield to the south.

Most of the Greylock Range is in the Mt. Greylock State Reservation, established in 1898 and now about 12,000 acres. From north to south the mountains are Mt. Prospect (2,690 feet), Mt. Williams (2,951 feet), Mt. Fitch (3,110 feet), Mt. Greylock (3,491 feet) and Saddle Ball Mountain (3,234 feet).

The Hopper, a bowl-shaped valley named for its resemblance to a grain hopper, is on the western side of Greylock. From its base the heavily wooded slopes rise steeply for over 1,500 feet. Designated as a National Natural Landmark in 1986, it contains a stand of old growth hemlock and beautiful cascading brooks.

Like virtually all New England mountains, old logging roads and numerous trails lace the range, including a 7.8 mile section of the Appalachian Trail that traverses north and south. Most of the forest is northern hardwood, but the upper slopes of Greylock and Saddle Ball, the two highest peaks, are covered with a boreal type forest of balsam fir and yellow birch, more similar to northern Canada than the rest of New England. In addition to common wildlife like white-tailed deer, ruffed grouse, raccoon, woodchucks and wild turkey, more than 40 state-listed rare or endangered species have been identified within the reservation.

The Department of Environmental Management (DEM) and the Appalachian Mountain Club maintain and manage facilities within the Reservation. This guide includes a description for every named trail within the Reservation (as of January 1999, each identified on the included map, *North Berkshire Trails*). The descriptions are roughly in order from closest to Williams College to most distant, subdivided into geographic areas: The Hopper, Greylock West, Greylock North, Greylock Summit, Greylock East and Greylock South.

New trails may be built and old trails closed or rerouted. Each year the DEM produces a current map free to all visitors. Pick one up or stop by the visitor center at Rockwell Road or Bascom Lodge at the summit with any questions.

It would be no small advantage if every college were located thus at the base of a mountain, as good at least as one well-endowed professorship...Some will remember, no doubt, not only that they went to college, but that they went to the mountain."

Henry David Thoreau
(Upon his visit to Mt. Greylock in 1847).

THE HOPPER

The Hopper is so named because of its resemblance to a grain chute when viewed from vantage points to the west, such as Route 7 near South Williamstown. Several trails ascend to high points of the Greylock Range from Money and Hopper Brooks.

MONEY BROOK TRAIL

Distances: 3.1 miles to Wilbur Clearing lean-to, 3.3 miles to the Appalachian Trail, 6.8 miles to Mt. Greylock summit.
Estimated time: 3.5 hours to summit.
Map location: I – 12.
Blazes: Blue.
Maintenance: Department of Environmental Management.

Coupled with the Appalachian Trail, the Money Brook Trail forms a long, picturesque route to the summit of Mt. Greylock. It also forms a nice circuit with either the Hopper or Prospect Mountain Trails. For much of its length, the trail follows first Hopper Brook and then Money Brook, veering away from them only in the last mile. Money Brook is named for the band of counterfeiters who are said to have used it as their hideout, and whose ghosts were later believed to haunt the surrounding woods.

HOW TO GET THERE
- From the junction of Routes 2 and 7, take Route 2 east to Route 43.
- Take Route 43 (Water St.) south to the Mt. Hope Park entrance (2.7 mi.).
- Turn left on Hopper Road. At a fork (4.1 mi.) bear left as black-top gives way to dirt.
- At the end of the dirt road, use the designated parking on the right. There is an information board with a map of the Greylock Reservation and other information.

DESCRIPTION

Just east of the parking area (0.0 mi.) the trail begins at a locked metal gate across the entrance to an old farm road that once extended into the Hopper. Skirting both this gate and a second one slightly further on, the trail continues along the road between maintained fields.

After the **Hopper Trail** diverges right, the Money Brook Trail continues to follow the wood road, coming out into a level field alongside Hopper Brook. This is a dispersed camping area.

Continue through the field and young wood beyond to a spectacular bridge over the cascading Money Brook. On the opposite (north) bank, follow a road until it reaches a second bridge over Money Brook. About 100 feet beyond the bridge a cut-off marked with blue triangles leads south to the Hopper Trail.

Leave the brook and ascend a hill to the right before descending to cross a small tributary, which may be dry in late summer. Just after crossing Money Brook (1.5 mi.), the **Mt. Prospect Trail** veers off to the left.

From here the Money Brook Trail follows the stream, but never crosses it. As you gradually gain elevation above the brook, cross a small tributary (2.2 mi.) to a steeper section, eventually making a sharp left (2.5 mi.).

A side trail continues 0.1 mi. straight to Money Brook Falls, a worthwhile diversion, especially in spring. The main trail climbs steeply out of the gorge, and you quickly lose the sound of the stream. At a level section, the Money Brook Cut-off leads 0.3 mi. east to **Notch Road**.

The Money Brook Trail continues through a stand of spruce, crosses a brook that is dry during the fall (3.1 mi.) and immediately passes a trail leading west to the Wilbur Clearing Lean-to. This sturdy, floored shelter sleeps six persons, but water may be a problem during the dry season. It was named for Jeremiah Wilbur, one of the original settlers in the Greylock area, who at one time farmed a 1,600-acre area stretching from **Bellows Pipe** over the top of Mt. Williams.

Just beyond the shelter the Money Brook Trail terminates at an intersection with the **Appalachian Trail** (3.3 mi.). To the left the AT leads up Prospect Mountain, to the right are Notch Road and the AT route over Mts. Williams, Fitch, and Greylock.

HALEY FARM TRAIL

Distance: 2.2 miles to Stony Ledge.
Estimated time: 2.0 hours.
Map location: I – 12.
Blazes: Blue.
Maintenance: Department of Environmental Management.

Haley and Greene farms have been active in the Hopper for centuries. The Commonwealth of Massachusetts, through the Department of Environmental Management (DEM), bought this land to protect access to the Hopper and Mt. Greylock Reservation in 1990. In 1997, the Williamstown Rural Lands Foundation and the DEM together cut the Haley Farm Trail to provide a new, short, steep route to Stony Ledge.

HOW TO GET THERE
• Refer to directions for the Money Brook Trail.

DESCRIPTION
Just east of the parking area is a locked metal gate across the entrance to an old farm road that once extended far into the Hopper. Skirting both this gate and a second one slightly further on, the trail continues along the road between maintained fields.

At the third gate, permanently open, the Haley Farm Trail leaves to the right (south). The **Money Brook Trail** and **Hopper Trail** continue straight ahead. From the stone wall (0.0 mi.), cross a field due south toward the treeline along a sparsely marked path. Enter the trees, and bear right to begin a gentle ascent. The open forest is dominated by tall, thin red maples, suggesting the recent history of agriculture. At the first of a series of switchbacks, the trail begins to climb much more steeply, broken up somewhat by a number of level stretches.

As you gain elevation the grade gradually eases through a large grove of juvenile birch and striped maple. After scrambling through and out of an old rocky gully, you join the **Stony Ledge Ski Trail** (1.8 mi.) for one final climb past the Stony Ledge shelter and campsite.

Finally, a breathtaking view from Stony Ledge rewards your perseverance. On a clear day it is possible to look down into the Hopper and up to the summits of Mt. Greylock, Fitch and Williams to the east. Prospect Mountain defines the opposite edge of the Hopper to the north.

HOPPER TRAIL

Distances: 2.4 miles to Sperry Road, 4.1 mi. to Greylock summit.
Estimated time: 2.5 hours to summit.
Map location: I – 12.
Blazes: Blue.
Maintenance: Department of Environmental Management.

On May 12, 1830 a group of over 100 people, a majority of them Williams students and faculty, left Haley's farm at the mouth of the Hopper and cut a trail to the summit of Mt. Greylock (according to "The American Advocate," a Williamstown newspaper of that day). The long history and direct route of the Hopper Trail make it one of the most hiked trails in the Mt. Greylock Reservation.

HOW TO GET THERE
• Refer to directions for the Money Brook Trail.

DESCRIPTION
Just east of the parking area is a locked metal gate across the entrance to an old farm road that once extended far into the Hopper. Skirting both this gate and a second one slightly further on, the trail continues along the road between maintained fields.

Just beyond a third gate that is permanently open, the **Haley Farm Trail** diverges to the right. After another hundred yards the Hopper Trail also bears off to the right, as the **Money Brook Trail** continues straight down the hill to a dispersed primitive camping area.

The Hopper Trail ascends through an overgrown pasture, scattered with wildflowers and a handful of twisted old apple trees. Enter the woods at the southeast corner of the field, and climb gently through an open forest. Through the trees to the left you can hear Hopper Brook, which cascades along the bottom of the valley, out of sight. The ascent steepens and you pass through an extensive grove of birch saplings and striped maple, before gradually leveling out in a red spruce forest near **Sperry Road**, just north of the campground (2.4 mi.).

Turn left and walk southeast along Sperry Road and along a bend to the right (south). Look for the Hopper Trail to the left heading east toward the summit. Almost immediately after crossing a stream for the second time, the trail arrives at a T-intersection with an old wood road. To the right is an extension of the **Deer Hill Trail**. The Hopper Trail takes a left onto the wood road, crosses the stream for a third time and enters a spruce grove.

Continue upward and cross two small streams. At a sharp right turn, the **Overlook Trail** descends to the left. Stay on the Hopper Trail; it will soon parallel **Rockwell Road**. The trail ends with the intersection at Rockwell Road (3.2 mi.). Follow the road 30 yards east to where it crosses the **Appalachian Trail** (AT), and continue north on the AT to the Mt. Greylock Summit (3.9 mi.).

MT. PROSPECT TRAIL

Distance: 4.0 miles to Appalachian Trail from Hopper trailhead.
Estimated time: 3 hours.
Map location: K – 12.
Blazes: Blue.
Maintenance: Department of Environmental Management.

The Mt. Prospect Trail is one of the most difficult hikes in the Greylock Reservation, but it is also one of the most beautiful, offering breathtaking views of the Hopper, the "Purple Valley," and the Taconic Range. Together with the Appalachian and Money Brook Trails, it makes an attractive 7.8 mi. loop

HOW TO GET THERE
• Refer to directions for the Money Brook Trail.

DESCRIPTION

Take the **Money Brook Trail** from Haley's Farm. 1.7 mi. from the trailhead, just after it crosses Money Brook for the last time, the Prospect Mountain Trail diverges to the left.

Leave the Money Brook Trail, and climb gradually up the northwest side of the ravine to the sharp ridge of Prospect Mountain (2.2 mi.), which it follows to the summit (3.0 mi.). The steepness of this section of the trail is compensated for by frequent overlooks with spectacular views of the Hopper, on the western side of Mt. Greylock. Look for the large groves of red spruce about halfway up—these stands of 200 year old trees were designated a Natural National Landmark in 1987.

Although there is no view from the top of Mt. Prospect (2,690 feet), a rock cairn marking the summit lets you know your climb is at an end. The trail winds north along the ridge, through a forest of red maple, beech and yellow birch. After passing several viewpoints, the trail ultimately joins the **Appalachian Trail** (4.0 mi.).

The "Prospect Lookout" at the junction is one of the best views in the Greylock Range. The valleys of the **Green River** and **Hoosic River** unfold to the west, at the base of the **Taconic Range**, and the **Green Mountains** of Vermont rise to the northwest. In spring and fall, this is also an excellent place to watch migrating hawks sail past.

To return to the Haley Farm, follow the Appalachian Trail to the right (southwest). After 0.3 mi. turn right on the Money Brook Trail and follow it to the Hopper Trailhead (7.8 mi.).

GREYLOCK NORTH

Mt. Prospect and Mt. Williams rise prominently above Williamstown and the Hoosic River. The Appalachian Trail and several other trails climb this northern end of the Greylock Range a few miles southeast of Williams College.

APPALACHIAN TRAIL
LUCE ROAD TO MT. GREYLOCK

Distance: 5.2 miles to Mt. Greylock summit.
Estimated time: 3 hours.
Map location: L – 16.
Blazes: White.
Maintenance: Department of Environmental Management and Appalachian Mountain Club.

Although not the most direct route up Greylock, the many beautiful vistas afforded by this section of the Appalachian Trail (AT) more than compensate for the distance. Be prepared for a stiff climb from the start up Mt. Prospect, one of the steepest in the region. This route touches on all the major peaks of the Greylock Range: Mt. Prospect (2,690 feet), Mt. Williams (2,951 feet), Mt. Fitch (3,110 feet) and Mt. Greylock (3,491 feet).

HOW TO GET THERE
- From the junction of Routes 2 and 7, take Route 2 east towards North Adams.
- Turn right on Luce Road (1.4 mi.).
- Follow Luce Rd. past the steep dikes of the Williamstown reservoir (2.8 mi.).
- The AT crosses the road 0.4 mi. beyond the reservoir. Two pullouts allow parking for five to six vehicles.

DESCRIPTION

From Luce Rd. (0.0 mi.), the AT winds through a stand of hemlocks and ascends a ridge on the north slope of Mt. Prospect (0.4 mi.), becoming quite steep near the top. When you crest the ridge (1.5 mi.), it intersects the **Mt. Prospect Trail**, which continues straight ahead while the AT turns left. From here enjoy the precipitous view of Williamstown and the Pownal valley to the west.

Turn sharply left (east) towards Mt. Williams. The trail leaves Mt. Prospect Ridge and descends to meet the **Money Brook Trail** in a grove of towering red spruce, some as much as 130 years old. The Wilbur Clearing Shelter, which sleeps six people, is located 0.3 mi. south along this trail. Beyond the Money Brook Trail, you cross Wilbur Clearing and **Notch Road** and then ascend Mt. Williams, making several sharp turns. From the summit (2.7 mi.), you may see North Adams and the Hoosac Range, Haystack Mountain in Vermont and, on a clear day, Mt. Monadnock in New Hampshire. To the east of the trail, a granite marker denotes the Mt. Greylock Reservation boundary.

From the Mt. Williams summit, descend to a saddle (3.1 mi.). A cut-off (blue blazes) leads 0.2 mi. west to Notch Road and **Old Summit Road** at Money Brook. Cross an unusual outcropping of milky quartz, to an open, east-facing junction with the **Bellows Pipe Trail** and **Thunderbolt Trail** (3.3 mi.). After passing another side trail to Notch Road (in 0.2 mi.) and **Robinson Point Trail**, the trail climbs steeply and crosses **Rockwell Road**. At the top, just before the Mt. Greylock parking lot, there is an open shelter on the right not for overnight use. To reach the summit of Mt. Greylock, continue through the parking lot to the War Memorial Tower (5.2 mi.).

NOTCH ROAD

Distances: 8.4 miles to Rockwell Road, 9.1 miles to summit.
Estimated time: 30 minutes driving.
Map location: N – 17.
Blazes: None.
Maintenance: Department of Environmental Management.

The former Braytonville Carriage Road is a hard-surfaced road that provides auto access to Greylock's summit during the summer months. It can be used to reach the Money Brook, Overlook, Robinson's Point and Appalachian Trails. During the winter snowmobiles and cross-country skiers use the road.

HOW TO GET THERE
- From Field Park follow Route 2 east to Braytonville.
- After the second Hoosic River crossing, turn right on Notch Road (4.1 mi.).

DESCRIPTION
From Route 2 (0.0 mi.), Notch Road travels south to the intersection with Pattison Road, where it makes a sharp left (1.3 mi.) at the Mt. Williams Reservoir. Pass through dense pine forest and then open fields to reach an intersection with Reservoir Road near a lone farmhouse at the base of Mt. Williams (2.4 mi.). From this junction, the **Bellows Pipe Trail** goes straight, while West Mountain Road, no longer passable by auto, leads left to Adams and North Adams. Notch Road continues to the west (right).

As you enter the Greylock Reservation (3.0 mi.) the **Bernard Farm Trail** starts to the right and Notch Road passes a piped spring to the east. At the low point in the saddle between Mt. Williams and Mt. Prospect, you intersect the **Appalachian Trail** (4.4 mi.). Limited day-parking is available at this crossing. Continue the ascent past the Money Brook Cut-off (5.1 mi.), a 0.2 mi. shortcut which connects with the **Money Brook Trail**. At the point where Notch Road crosses Money Brook, a 0.2 mi. access trail leads east to the Appalachian Trail (AT).

The upper section of Notch Road offers several impressive views of the Hopper. Just south of the **Robinson's Point Trail**, there is a pullout on the west side of the road (7.4 mi.), across from a second cut-off to the AT. Although the trail itself can be somewhat difficult to find, it is easy to bushwhack the 0.1 mi. east to the AT in this area. Slightly beyond the pullout is the beginning of the **Overlook Trail** (7.5 mi.).

Notch Road continues to another AT crossing (8.4 mi.), where it joins **Rockwell Road** at another AT crossing. Rockwell Road spirals the final distance to Greylock summit (9.1 mi.).

CASCADES TRAIL

Distance: 1.0 mile (round-trip).
Estimated time: 45 minutes.
Blazes: None.
Map location: N – 17.
Maintenance: None.

Hidden in the middle of development, the Cascades is a beautiful waterfall in North Adams along Notch Brook.

HOW TO GET THERE
- From Field Park follow Route 2 east to Braytonville.
- After the second Hoosic River crossing and Notch Road, turn right on Marion Avenue (4.2 mi.).
- Follow Marion Ave. to the end and park on the right before a split rail fence. There is room for only 2-3 cars.

DESCRIPTION
The Cascades Trail is an extension of Marion Avenue, unused by vehicles in recent history. You follow Notch Brook and cross it a couple times. The Cascades (0.5 mi.) plunge about fifty feet where harder rock has eroded more slowly than the marble downstream. Notch brook originates in the **Bellows Pipe** between **Ragged Mountain** and Mt. Williams. Return the way you came (1.0 mi.).

BERNARD FARM TRAIL

Distance: 2.3 miles (approximately) to Appalachian Trail.
Estimated time: 2 hours.
Blazes: Blue.
Map location: N – 15.
Maintenance: Department of Environmental Management.

From Bernard Farm this trail connects a series of wood roads along-side Notch Road up the flank of Mt. Williams. It offers a direct route to the Appalachian Trail (AT) and the summit of Greylock.

HOW TO GET THERE

- Drive east on Route 2 from Routes 2 and 7 in Williamstown.
- After crossing the Hoosic for the second time, turn right (south) on Notch Road at a sign for Mt. Greylock State Reservation (4.1 mi.).
- At an intersection near Mt. Williams Reservoir, follow Notch Rd. to the left (east).
- At the next intersection, Notch Road turns right. The Bernard Farm and trailhead are also on the right.

DESCRIPTION

Harry Bernard ran a dairy farm on this site in the early part of this century. He also drove children to school with his "school team" before buses, extracted timber used for construction of Bascom Lodge in the 1930's and operated a small ski area in the 1940's and 1950's (*Most Excellent Majesty*).

From the farm and Mt. Greylock Reservation Boundary (0.0 mi.) follow an old wood road to the northwest. A series of trails and wood roads link up the mountainside, across **Notch Road** to the **Appalachian Trail** just south of Mt. Williams (2.3 mi.)

BELLOWS PIPE TRAIL

Distance: 4.0 miles.
Estimated time: 3.0 hours.
Blazes: Blue.
Map location: N – 14.
Maintenance: Department of Environmental Management.

Bellows Pipe, named for the roar of wind in this tight valley, was originally called the Notch; a name still held by the stream that flows down it and the road that accesses the area. Jeremiah Wilbur cleared a road up the Notch and on to the summit of Greylock in the late 18th Century. The Bellows Pipe Trail follows portions of this old route, and offers access to Ragged Mountain.

HOW TO GET THERE
- Drive east on Route 2 from Routes 2 and 7 in Williamstown.
- After crossing the Hoosic for the second time, turn right (south) on Notch Road.
- At an intersection by Mt. Williams Reservoir, follow Notch Rd. to the left (east).
- At the next intersection, Notch Road turns right and Bellows Pipe is directly ahead. There is parking by the trail head.

DESCRIPTION
From **Notch Road** (0.0 mi.), the trail follows an old wood road, maybe the route of Jeremiah Wilbur's original summit road. As you climb along Notch Brook, imagine an active farm with three mills along the brook, hayfields, gardens, orchards, a stand of sugar maple, cows and sheep.

At 2.2 mi. you reach the saddle between **Ragged Mountain** and Greylock's northeastern slope. Here a short trail to the left (east) leads to Ragged Mountain.

You cross a streambed and reach the Bellows Pipe Shelter before a trail junction (2.5 mi.). Straight ahead, an old grade intersects the **Thunderbolt Trail** and drops to the Gould Farm. Turn right onto steeper terrain with a series of switchbacks to the **Appalachian Trail** (AT) marked by white blazes.

Turn left on the AT, pass the top of the Thunderbolt and **Overlook Trails**, and climb gradually towards the summit. Cross the **Rockwell Road** just before the summit clearing and War Memorial (4.0 mi.).

RAGGED MOUNTAIN TRAIL

Distance: 0.4 mile (approximately).
Estimated time: 20 minutes.
Blazes: Blue.
Map location: M – 11.
Maintenance: Department of Environmental Management.

This short spur trail ascends to the summit of Ragged Mountain from the Bellows Pipe, also known as the Notch. In 1910 the Massachusetts State legislature authorized a trolley line from Adams to this point and onto the summit of Greylock. Three years later the proposal died.

HOW TO GET THERE
- Ascend the Bellows Pipe Trail or Thunderbolt Trail to the saddle between Ragged Mountain and Mt. Greylock.
- Alternatively, descend the Appalachian Trail and Bellows Pipe Trail from the summit of Greylock.

DESCRIPTION
From the **Bellows Pipe Trail** (0.0 mi.) in the saddle near the Bellows Pipe Shelter, follow a spur trail to the east. You climb a winding and steep route to the summit of Ragged Mountain in about twenty minutes (0.4 mi.). From here are excellent views south to Mt. Greylock, Saddle Ball Mountain and Greylock Glen.

OLD SUMMIT ROAD

Distance: 0.8 mile (approximately).
Estimated time: 25 minutes.
Blazes: Blue.
Map location: L – 14.
Maintenance: Department of Environmental Management.

Named for a historic road up Greylock, this trail bypasses the summit of Mt. Williams between sections of Notch Road and the Appalachian Trail.

HOW TO GET THERE
- Most will use this trail as a convenient cut-off when hiking the Appalachian Trail (AT).
- By car: refer to directions and description for Notch Road. Park at the AT crossing 1.4 mi. from the Reservation boundary.

DESCRIPTION
Head southeast from the **Appalachian Trail** day-use parking area. Along the way you will pass signed cut-offs to the AT, **Notch Road** and **Money Brook Trail**. Near the junction with the AT and **Bernard Farm Trail** a chimney marks the site of the Williams Outing Club Harris Memorial Cabin built in 1932 and mysteriously burned on Halloween night in 1961.

GREYLOCK WEST

South of the Hopper a couple of trails climb up Goodell Hollow to Sperry Road on Stony Ledge. There several short trails visit the cascades of March Cataract Falls and the Heart of Greylock.

ROARING BROOK TRAIL

Distance: 1.9 miles.
Estimated time: 1.5 hours.
Map location: H – 10.
Blazes: Blue.
Maintenance: Department of Environmental Management.

The Roaring Brook and Stony Ledge Trails form an excellent six-mile loop to views of the Hopper and Greylock Range from Stony Ledge. Many prefer to hike up the steep Stony Ledge Trail and descend the more gradual Roaring Brook Trail. You may also use either trail to reach the summit of Greylock and other trails in the park.

HOW TO GET THERE
- Take Route 7 south from Field Park in Williamstown.
- 1.6 mi. after the junction with Route 43 in South Williamstown, turn left on Roaring Brook Road (5.7 mi. total)
- Drive 0.5 mi. to a sign for the Mt. Greylock Ski Club and a pullout on the left. The road is private beyond this point, so all cars should be parked here.

DESCRIPTION
Start on the wood road to the left, along Roaring Brook (0.0 mi.). You cross Roaring Brook, ascend slightly, and then descend to cross the brook again. Proceed through the meadow on the south side of the stream, bear left at a split in the dirt road and make a third crossing of Roaring Brook.

At 0.5 mi. the Roaring Brook Trail and **Stony Ledge Trail** diverge on the north side of Roaring Brook. From here, you leave the brook and rapidly ascend through a mixture of evergreen and deciduous trees to a spruce grove, where the grade finally flattens out (1.6 mi.).

Just before a bridge over Roaring Brook (1.8 mi.), the **Deer Hill Trail** leaves to the right. On the other side of the Bridge the **Circular Trail** heads downhill. Continue parallel to the brook for another 200 yards and enter Sperry Campground. There are picnic tables, campsites and group shelters (fee and reservation) here.

Turn left (north) and cross a bridge over a small stream. The Roaring Brook Trail follows a wood road to intersect with Sperry Road (1.9 mi.) and the **Hopper Trail**. The summit of Greylock is 2.3 mi. along the Hopper Trail (4.2 mi. total).

For a spectacular view of the entire Greylock Reservation, turn left on Sperry Road and walk 1.0 mi. up to the Stony Ledge picnic area (3.0 mi.). Straight across from the ledge (east) is the Greylock summit, and to the left are Mt. Fitch, Mt. Williams and Mt. Prospect. Stony Ledge is the site of **Mountain Day**, the Williams Outing Club's annual celebration of the fall foliage.

You can return to Roaring Brook Road via the Stony Ledge Trail (5.1 mi.), but it is a much steeper descent than the Roaring Brook Trail. Otherwise retrace your steps, or continue over the range to a car shuttle.

STONY LEDGE TRAIL

Distance: 2.1 miles.
Estimated time: 1.5 hours.
Map location: H – 10.
Blazes: Blue.
Maintenance: Department of Environmental Management.

The Civilian Conservation Corps (CCC) built the Stony Ledge Ski Trail in the 1930s but it has not been maintained for skiing recently. This steep climb ends with magnificent views across the Hopper from Stony Ledge. Descend the Roaring Brook Trail for a 5.1-mile loop.

HOW TO GET THERE

• Refer to directions for the Roaring Brook Trail.

DESCRIPTION

Start on the wood road to the left, along Roaring Brook (0.0 mi.). You cross Roaring Brook, ascend slightly, and then descend to cross the brook again. Proceed through the meadow on the south side of the stream, bear left at a split in the dirt road and make a third crossing of Roaring Brook.

At 0.5 mi. the **Roaring Brook Trail** and Stony Ledge Trail diverge on the north side of Roaring Brook. Follow an old wood road on a gradual climb to the north. At 1.2 mi. the trail swings right (east) onto the steep part of the old ski trail.

You crest the ridge near a lean-to and continue to the lookout from Stony Ledge (2.1 mi.). Here you can see (from left to right) **Prospect Mountain**, Mt. Williams, Mt. Fitch, Mt. Greylock and part of Saddle Ball Mountain.

SPERRY ROAD

Distance: 1.7 miles to Stony Ledge.
Estimated time: 5 minutes driving.
Blazes: None.
Map location: J – 9.
Maintenance: Department of Environmental Management.

Sperry Road provides access to Sperry Campground, Stony Ledge and several trails from Rockwell Road. The Civilian Conservation Corps based its Greylock crew here in the 1930s.

HOW TO GET THERE

• Refer to description for Rockwell Road.
• Sperry Road leaves Rockwell Road 6.3 mi. from Quarry Road.

DESCRIPTION

Sperry Road leads 0.6 mi. to Sperry Campground and 1.7 mi. to Stony Ledge. Sperry Campground was a farm site in the late 1700's.

In 1863 the Williams Alpine Club established a camping area there. Later, the Civilian Conservation Corps based its operations and 200 men at the same site. Currently, it is open to the public for a fee from May to October and free during the winter months when there is no auto access.

Parking near the entrance station provides access to the **Hopper Trail**, **March Cataract Trail**, **Circular Loop**, **Deer Hill Trail** and **Roaring Brook Trail**. Sperry Road ends on the summit of Stony Ledge, just north of a shelter and the **Stony Ledge Trail**, with a view that encompasses the entire Greylock Range.

CIRCULAR TRAIL

Distance: 0.6 miles (approximately).
Estimated time: 25 minutes.
Blazes: Blue.
Map location: J – 10.
Maintenance: Department of Environmental Management.

The Circular Trail provides a short loop walk from Sperry Campground.

HOW TO GET THERE
- Go to Sperry Campground. On foot the Hopper and Roaring Brook Trail provide the most direct access. By car use Notch Road or Rockwell to Sperry Road, all described in this book.
- The Circular Trail begins with the Roaring Brook Trail at a bend in Sperry Road near the group fee shelters and entry station at the southeast end of the campground.

DESCRIPTION
Start along the **Roaring Brook Trail** heading south from **Sperry Road.** At the first footbridge, the Circular Trail leaves to the left (south) side of the brook. Follow the loop back around to the Roaring Brook Trail and turn right to return to Sperry Road.

DEER HILL TRAIL

Distance: 2.0 miles (loop).
Estimated time: 1 hour 15 minutes.
Blazes: Blue.
Map location: J – 10.
Maintenance: Department of Environmental Management.

This pleasant loop high on Mt. Greylock starts and ends at Sperry Campground. Along the way are Deer Hill Falls, a shelter and an old carriage road. The Civilian Conservation Corps built this trail to what Williams College professor Albert Hopkins called the "Heart of Greylock," A stand of old growth hemlock at the falls.

HOW TO GET THERE

- Go to Sperry Campground. On foot the Hopper and Roaring Brook Trail provide the most direct access. By car use Notch Road or Rockwell Road to Sperry Road, all described in this book.
- The Deer Hill Trail begins with the Roaring Brook Trail at a bend in Sperry Road near the group fee shelters and entry station at the southeast end of the campground.

DESCRIPTION

Start on the **Roaring Brook Trail** heading southwest from Sperry Road (0.0 mi.). Soon you leave the Roaring Brook Trail (0.1 mi.) and descend to Deer Hill Falls before a greater climb up past a shelter (0.8 mi.) towards **Rockwell Road** (southeast). Turn left on a carriage road and left again on Sperry Road to return to the trailhead (2.0 mi.).

MARCH CATARACT TRAIL

Distance: 0.8 miles from Sperry Campground to falls.
Estimated time: 25 minutes (one-way).
Blazes: Blue.
Map location: J – 10.
Maintenance: Department of Environmental Management.

For a short hike from Sperry Campground, try the March Cataract Trail to Bacon Brook, a tributary of Hopper Brook.

HOW TO GET THERE

- Go to Sperry Campground. On foot the Hopper and Roaring Brook Trail provide the most direct access, although any trail to the summit area of Greylock will do. By car use Notch Road or Rockwell Road to Sperry Road, all described in this book.
- March Cataract Trail begins at a bend in Sperry Road near the group fee shelters and entry station at the southeast end of the campground.

DESCRIPTION

From **Sperry Road** (0.0 mi.) follow the trail gradually up and then more steeply down into the upper reaches of the Hopper. Farther north on this steep terrain are areas of old-growth forest spared by their inaccessibility. At 0.8 mi. you reach March Cataract Falls on the upper reaches of Hopper Brook. Spring is the best time to see the cascades, when snowmelt and swollen groundwater supplies run down the mountain. Return the way you came.

Greylock Range–View from North atop Pine Cobble.

GREYLOCK SUMMIT

Trails from all around converge at the 3,491 foot summit of Mt. Greylock. The Overlook and Robinson Point Trails provide a tour of the summit area with fantastic viewpoints. Basom Lodge and the War Memorial offer visitor facilities for hikers and tourists.

OVERLOOK TRAIL

Distance: Part of a 2.7 mile loop from the Mt. Greylock summit.
Estimated time: 1.5 hours.
Map location: L – 11.
Blazes: Blue.
Maintenance: Department of Environmental Management.

Bypassing the summit of Mt. Greylock, this trail connects the Hopper Trail on the south with the Appalachian Trail on the north. On a clear day, it affords views of the Hopper that are not possible from any other trail or summit. Link the Overlook, Hopper, and Appalachian Trails and the Old Carriage Road to make a pleasant 2.7 mile circuit from the Greylock summit. Although the trail is not steep, portions of it do require scrambling over tree roots and rocks.

HOW TO GET THERE
  • You must be in the summit area of Mt. Greylock for this trail. Use any of the hiking trails from surrounding valleys, Notch Road or Rockwell Road to ascend the mountain.
  • Park at the summit or the first two day-use parking areas along Rockwell Road. The description starts from the summit of Greylock, but you may pick up the loop anywhere along the way.

DESCRIPTION

Start at the Mt. Greylock parking lot and descend the Old Carriage Road. The road starts at the southeast corner of the Radio Tower building near the exit, but the sign is only visible if you are facing south on the AT. After 0.5 mi. the trail makes a sharp left to meet and cross **Notch Road**.

From Notch Road, the trail levels out and follows the contours of the mountain. You pass through a stand of conifers and continue to the first overlook, located down a 20 yard side trail to the right. **Stony Ledge** is visible to the left, the south side of **Prospect Mountain** to the right, and the **Taconic Range** in the distance.

After crossing a stream and a swampy area forested with balsam and hemlock, the trail approaches a second overlook, again down a short side trail to the right.

Somewhat further on, the trail crosses Bacon Brook upstream of **March Cataract Falls**. Climb back up to the Hopper Trail and **Rockwell Road** (1.7 mi.) To return to the Greylock summit, follow the **Hopper Trail** east (left) to Rockwell Road. Join the AT where it intersects Rockwell Road (2.1 mi.), and follow it northeast to the Greylock parking lot (2.7 mi.). To reach Sperry Campground, Stony Ledge and the **Money Brook** trailhead, follow the Hopper Trail down to the right.

ROBINSON POINT TRAIL

Distance: 0.2 mile.
Estimated time: 5-10 minutes.
Blazes: Blue
Map location: L – 11.
Maintenance: Department of Environmental Management.

A fantastic view west into the Hopper and across to the Taconic Range may be had with a short walk from Notch Road.

HOW TO GET THERE

- Refer to directions for Notch Road. 7.4 mi. from Route 2, or 4.4 mi. from the Reservation entrance, park in a pullout on the right (west side of the road).

DESCRIPTION

Follow the short but very steep trail down to a spectacular overlook above the Hopper. To the right is Prospect Mountain; to the left is Stony Ledge.

BASCOM LODGE

After a summit log cabin burned in 1929, the State of Massachusetts and the Civilian Conservation Corps built the more grand Bascom Lodge to match summit houses on other New England Peaks. Completed in 1937, it is constructed of native stone and timber with lodging, a dining room, staff quarters, a common room and a trading post (*Most Excellent Majesty*). Since 1983 the Appalachian Mountain Club (AMC) has managed the lodge along with naturalist and trail crew programs. Contact the AMC to reserve lodging at Bascom Lodge.

WAR MEMORIAL

As plans for Bascom Lodge took shape, the form of a new tower rose on Mt. Greylock where an old iron structure and the original wooden towers had stood before. The 92-foot tall granite memorial was built to honor Massachusetts men and women who died in World War I. Originally designed to be a lighthouse memorial in Boston Harbor, the structure was built instead on the summit in the 1930s. At that time, twelve powerful searchlights made the tower a beacon visible for seventy miles! Over time the fierce mountain weather has necessitated several major repairs of the tower, most recently for the Mt. Greylock State Reservation centennial in 1998. From an observation area high in the tower you can see for over one hundred miles on a clear day.

GREYLOCK EAST

From the Town of Adams a number of trails climb the steep east side of Mt. Greylock from Greylock Glen. A development called Greylock Center may change trails and access routes at Greylock Glen in the near future.

CHESHIRE HARBOR TRAIL

Distances: 2.6 miles to Rockwell Road, 3.3 miles to summit.
Estimated time: 2 hours to summit.
Map location: M – 7.
Blazes: Blue.
Maintenance: Department of Environmental Management.

This trail is the easiest, most direct route to the summit of Greylock, in part because it begins at a relatively high elevation. Every Columbus Day, hundreds of hikers ascend this way during the Greylock Ramble, an event sponsored by the Adams Chamber of Commerce. The trail is named for a historic town site where Basset Brook meets modern Route 8. Although it suggests proximity to a large body of water, the name actually refers to the fact that it is reported to have been a stop on the underground railroad.

HOW TO GET THERE
- Drive east on Route 2 from Williamstown.
- As you enter North Adams (5.0 mi.) follow signs to Downtown, Route 8 south and Heritage State Park; bear right to Main Street and a stop light.
- Take Route 8 south (5.1 mi.).
- At the Monument to President McKinley in Adams, turn right (west) onto Maple St. (10.4 mi.).
- Pass a cemetery and turn left on West Road (10.8 mi.).
- After another 0.5 mi. turn right on West Mountain Road (11.3 mi. total) at a sign for Greylock Greenhouses.
- Follow for 1.6 mi. to a dead-end at the trailhead, clearly marked with a sign (12.9 mi.).

DESCRIPTION

This wide and easy-to-follow trail climbs steadily up an old woods road, passing several old stone foundations. At the first switchback, it intersects a trail to the **Gould Trail** trailhead (0.4 mi.). After two more switchbacks, the Cheshire Harbor Trail diverges from the wood road (1.0 mi.), bearing off to the right and up while the wood road bears left, becoming **Old Adams Road**.

Old Adams Road connects to the **Appalachian Trail** (AT) in approximately 1.7 miles. On a clear day, the summit of Mt. Greylock should become visible as you ascend, with the memorial tower rising over Peck's Brook ravine.

The Cheshire Harbor Trail continues to the northwest, through stands of northern hardwoods that have been severely stressed by atmospheric pollution. Scientists have designated several plots in the area to study the decline of high altitude forests in New England, and the number of dead trees suggests that the problem may be quite serious.

Just after the trail crosses Pecks Brook (2.3 mi.), it terminates at **Rockwell Road** (2.6 mi.), also the junction with the AT. From here, the summit of Mt. Greylock is 0.7 mi. north along the AT.

OLD ADAMS ROAD

Distances: 2.8 miles, Cheshire Harbor Trail to Appalachian Trail, 4.8 miles to Rockwell Road.
Estimated time: 1.5 hours to Appalachian Trail.
Map location: L – 8.
Blazes: Blue.
Maintenance: Department of Environmental Management.

Old Adams Road connects the Cheshire Harbor Trail, Appalachian Trail, and Rockwell Road on the southeast side of the Greylock range. It follows a near-level grade around Saddle Ball Mountain.

HOW TO GET THERE

- Refer to directions for the Cheshire Harbor Trail.
- Follow the Cheshire Harbor Trail for 1.0 mi. to the third switchback and then bear left (south) onto a wood road grade.

DESCRIPTION

After leaving the **Cheshire Harbor Trail** (0.0 mi.), Old Adams Road heads east, crossing a bridge over the first of a series of brooks (0.2 mi.). The bridge over the second brook (0.8 mi.) is at the base of an attractive waterfall.

Continue past a lesser used wood road that branches left toward Cheshire (1.7 mi.), and then cross three more brooks. At the next intersection (2.7 mi.), **Redgate Road** drops to the southeast. Old Adams Road continues west to an intersection with the **Appalachian Trail** (2.8 mi.). Kitchen Brook is just south of the junction.

Old Adams Road continues another 2.0 mi. around the south end of Saddle Ball Mountain to **Rockwell Road** at the **Jones' Nose** parking area (4.8 mi.).

GOULD TRAIL

Distances: 3.0 miles to Rockwell Road, 3.4 miles to summit.
Estimated time: 2.5 hours.
Blazes: Blue.
Map location: M – 8.
Maintenance: Department of Environmental Management.

One of several trails from the Adams side of Greylock, the Gould Trail climbs about 1700 feet of elevation in three miles. Along the way is Pecks Brook shelter, a beautiful spot to spend a night on Mt. Greylock.

HOW TO GET THERE

- Drive east on Route 2 from Williamstown.
- As you enter North Adams (5.0 mi.) follow signs to Downtown, Route 8 south and Heritage State Park; bear right to Main Street and a stop light.
- Take Route 8 south (5.1 mi.).
- At the Monument to President McKinley in Adams, turn right (west) onto Maple St. (10.4 mi.).
- Pass a cemetery and turn left on West Road (10.8 mi.).
- After another 0.5 mi. turn right on West Mountain Road (11.3 total) at a sign for Greylock Greenhouses.

• Follow for 0.9 mi. to a trailhead on the right, clearly marked with a sign (12.2 mi.).

DESCRIPTION

From West Mountain Road (0.0 mi.) enter the woods at the south end of the field. At the first junction head north (right); straight ahead a trail links up with the **Cheshire Harbor Trail**. After a short, gradual descent to a second junction, turn left (west) and begin your climb in earnest.

You ascend just north of Pecks Brook to a cut-off to the Cheshire Harbor Trail south of the brook. At 2.0 mi. a short side trail leads to Pecks Brook Shelter along the stream. Another mi. of steady climbing brings you to the **Rockwell Road** (3.0 mi.). From the intersection of Notch and Rockwell Roads follow the **Appalachian Trail** to the summit (3.4 mi.).

REDGATE ROAD

Distance: 2.2 miles (approximately).
Estimated time: 1.5 hours.
Blazes: Blue.
Map location: M – 7.
Maintenance: Department of Environmental Management.

Many trails in the North Berkshire area utilize old wood roads or turnpikes. Redgate Road is one, in places deeply gullied from use as a route from Adams to New Ashford and Lanesboro in the 1800s.

HOW TO GET THERE

• Refer to directions for the Cheshire Harbor Trail.

DESCRIPTION

From the **Cheshire Harbor Trail** trailhead, follow the abandoned continuation of West Mountain Road. After about 0.4 mi., the Redgate road leaves to the right (west), just before Bassett Brook. The grade is obvious and a single blaze has been chopped in the bark of a sixteen inch tree.

Soon you will cross a bridge, then turn left (southeast), off a wood road to cross another bridge. Climb slowly up a small valley west of Cole Mountain. At the head to this valley follow the trail as it swings west and northwest to meet **Old Adams Road** near the **Appalachian Trail** (AT) after about 2.2 miles.

From here you have a number of options. You could follow the AT to Saddle Ball Mountain and Mt. Greylock or use the Old Adams Road to return via the Cheshire Harbor Trail, among others.

SILVERFOX TRAIL

Distance: 1.3 miles (approximately).
Estimated time: 1 hour.
Blazes: Blue.
Map location: M – 7.
Maintenance: Department of Environmental Management.

This trail provides a route from Redgate Road to Old Adams Road.

HOW TO GET THERE
• Refer to directions for the Cheshire Harbor Trail.

DESCRIPTION
From the **Cheshire Harbor Trail** trailhead, follow the abandoned continuation of West Mountain Road. After about 0.4 mi., the **Redgate Road** leaves to the right (west), just before Bassett Brook, follow it. The grade is obvious and a single blaze has been chopped in the bark of a sixteen-inch tree.

Soon you will cross a bridge. The Silverfox Trail continues straight ahead while the Redgate Road turns left and crosses a second bridge. This new trail is used mostly by snowmobiles in winter and may be difficult to follow.

From Redgate Road it is about 1.3 mi. to **Old Adams Road**. There you may turn right to reach the Cheshire Harbor Trail or left to the **Appalachian Trail**.

THUNDERBOLT TRAIL

Distance: 1.6 miles to Appalachian Trail.
Estimated time: 2.0 hours.
Blazes: Blue.
Map location: N – 10.
Maintenance: Department of Environmental Management.

Skiing as a sport did not gain popularity in the United States until the 1930s. The Mount Greylock Ski Club fueled its growth in the Berkshires and helped lay out the Thunderbolt Ski Trail. In the fall of 1934, thirty Civilian Conservation Corps members cleared this 1.6-mile trail 2,175 vertical feet down the east side of Mt. Greylock.

Skiers competed in sanctioned races on the Thunderbolt trail through the mid-1950s. In 1948 Per Klippgen set the record of two minutes and nine seconds, top to bottom, an average speed of about 45 miles per hour! After years of little maintenance trees have grown in and most hike the Thunderbolt Trail today (*Most Excellent Majesty*).

HOW TO GET THERE
- Drive east on Route 2 from Williamstown.
- As you enter North Adams (5.0 mi.) follow signs to Downtown, Route 8 south and Heritage State Park; bear right to Main Street and a stoplight.
- Take Route 8 south (5.1 mi.).
- At the Monument to President McKinley in Adams, turn right (west) onto Maple St. (10.4 mi.).
- Pass a cemetery and turn left after 0.4 mi. on West Road (10.8 mi.).
- After another 0.4 mi. turn right on Gould Road (11.2 mi. total) at a sign for Greylock Glen.
- Follow Gould Road for 0.4 mi. and then continue straight on Thiel Road where Gould Road turns left (11.6 mi.).
- Drive 0.5 mi. to a trailhead, marked with a sign for the Thunderbolt Trail and Bellows Pipe (12.1 mi.). If you cross a minor brook (Hoxie) you have gone too far.

DESCRIPTION

From Thiel Road, follow the right (north) of two trails, a dirt road along the south side of Hoxie Brook. You will pass a turn-off to the left, then arrive at a sharp switchback, also to the left. A trail goes right across Hoxie Brook toward **Ragged Mountain** to the north, turn left.

There is a switchback in the trail right after contouring under a very steep slope. As you climb, you follow the steep valley of Hoxie Brook. At the next intersection, a spur trail to the left takes you to a lookout and berries in late summer. Back on the Thunderbolt Trail, keep climbing along Hoxie Brook to a junction with the **Bellows Pipe Trail**.

To the left, the Bellows Pipe Extension leads down to Gould Farm on a more gentle grade, a better descent route than the lower Thunderbolt Trail. From here you climb a ridiculously steep grade, with the famous drops and turns ski racers negotiated: Big Bend, the Needle, the Big Schuss and the Schuss. At 1.6 mi. you crest at the **Appalachian Trail** (1.6 mi.). Turn left on the AT to reach the Greylock Summit (2.0 mi.).

GREYLOCK GLEN

To access the trails described in Greylock East, you must pass through Greylock Glen, a part of the Mt. Greylock State Reservation above the town of Adams.

For thirty years this mostly level piece of land has been targeted for development by the state, county, and town of Adams to compensate for the decline of industry in the area. Proposals for a tramway, ski area, golf course, hotel and residential development have come and gone in the past forty years.

As of 1999 the Greylock Center is the latest development proposal. An environmental center, golf course, trail network, cross country ski area, conference center and lodging are all aspects of the current plan. Although much time and effort have been invested in this project, the date of construction is unknown.

Be aware that trailheads, trails and facilities in Greylock Glen may change after publication of this edition.

GREYLOCK SOUTH

Rockwell Road and several trails provide convenient access to Mt. Greylock along Saddle Ball Mountain from the south A visitor center at the Reservation entrance has maps, information and restrooms.

ROCKWELL ROAD

Distance: 8.5 miles to Greylock summit.
Estimated time: 20 minutes driving from Visitors Center.
Map location: H – 1 (Beginning off map).
Blazes: None.
Maintenance: Department of Environmental Management.

Since its construction in 1906-7, Rockwell Road has been the most used auto road to the summit of Mt. Greylock. From the park Visitor Center to Greylock's summit, the road provides access to many trails and park facilities. In winter months Rockwell Road is unplowed and used as a snowmobile trail.

HOW TO GET THERE
- Take Route 7 south toward Pittsfield from Williamstown.
- After 13.3 mi. and brown signs for the Visitor Center and Bascom Lodge, turn left on North Main Street.
- Bear right onto Quarry Road at 15.1 miles. A sign directs you to "State Reservation".
- Next bear left on Rockwell Road (15.5 mi.) by the maintenance facility and enter the Mt. Greylock State Reservation.

DESCRIPTION
From Quarry Road (0.0 mi.), Rockwell Road begins its 8.5-mile ascent of Mt. Greylock. At 0.6 mi. you pass the Visitors Center on the right. Inside is a wealth of print information as well as a friendly staff from the Department of Environmental Management and the Appalachian Mountain Club to answer questions. In winter a gate

closes the road to vehicles beyond this point.

From the visitor center parking you may access the short **Brook and Berry Trail** and **Cliff Trail** in all seasons. Rockwell Road passes through private land for a short stretch and reenters the Reservation at about 2.0 miles. The **Northrup Trail** leaves to the left (west). This trail is used mostly for skiing in winter. Use the **Jones' Nose** parking in summer.

A gravel pullout on the right (east) at 3.7 mi. is parking for the **Rounds' Rock Trail**. Further along you reach the Jones' Nose day parking area (4.4 mi.) with access to the Northrup Trail, Jones' Nose Trail, **CCC Dynamite Trail**, **Appalachian Trail** (AT), and **Old Adams Road**.

After a straight and level stretch **Greylock Road** enters from the left (5.6 mi.). This steep dirt road connects to Route 7. Slightly further up the mountain, **Sperry Road** (6.3 mi.) bears left from Rockwell Road.

Rockwell Road begins to climb more steeply from Sperry Road toward the summit. The **Overlook Trail** begins where the road makes a hairpin turn (7.2 mi.). The **Hopper Trail** is also accessible at this point. A second switchback (7.3 mi.) coincides with the AT. Just beyond this, Rockwell Road intersects both the AT and the end of the **Cheshire Harbor Trail**.

Notch Road enters from the northwest (left) at a third crossing of the AT (7.8 mi.). From this junction, Rockwell Road circles Mt. Greylock to the summit (8.5 mi.).

BROOK AND BERRY TRAIL

Distances: 2.0 miles (loop).
Estimated time: 1 hour.
Blazes: Blue.
Map location: H – 1.
Maintenance: Department of Environmental Management.

A leisurely two-mile loop from the Mt. Greylock Reservation Visitor Center includes the Brook and Berry Trail as well as the Cliff Trail west of Rockwell Road.

HOW TO GET THERE
- Refer to directions for Rockwell Road.
- Park at the Visitor Center (16.0 mi.).

DESCRIPTION

Follow signs at the far (east) end of the parking lot into the woods onto a clear path. Walk north by a brook along either the summer or winter trail to **Rockwell Road** (1.0 mile).

Return the same way, or cross the road to the Cliff Trail and return south to the Visitor Center (2.0 mi.).

ROUNDS' ROCK TRAIL

Distance: 0.7 miles (loop).
Estimated time: 30 minutes.
Blazes: Blue.
Map location: I – 5.
Maintenance: Department of Environmental Management.

In 1915, the Greylock Commission purchased Rounds' Rock (2,580) and "the finest view of the larger portion of the county anywhere to be obtained" (*Most Excellent Majesty*). A short walk from Rockwell Road rewards you with fantastic views of cliffs to the south and west.

HOW TO GET THERE
- Refer to directions for Rockwell Road.
- Drive 3.1 mi. past the visitor center to a gravel pullout on the right before the Jones' Nose parking.

DESCRIPTION

Carefully cross **Rockwell Road** (0.0 mi.) and enter the forest. Jabez Rounds grazed sheep and tended orchards here in the 1790s. Low bush blackberries peak in August for your picking pleasure.

At the outer end of the loop two spur trails lead to vistas of the Catskills, Connecticut and Mt. Monadnock (west to east) on a clear day. A memorial marks the site of a 1945 plane crash. Follow the loop or retrace your steps to Rockwell Road (0.7 mi.).

NORTHRUP TRAIL

Distance: 3.0 miles.
Estimated time: 1.5 hours.
Blazes: Blue.
Map location: I – 6.
Maintenance: Department of Environmental Management.

This level trail shares parking with the Jones' Nose Trail and Old Adams Road. It provides easy access to the short trails and views of Rounds' Rock to the south. In winter it provides a route for skiers to avoid snowmobiles on Rockwell Road.

HOW TO GET THERE
- Refer to directions for Rockwell Road.
- Drive past the visitor center, into the park, past Rounds' Rock to the Jones' Nose Trailhead.

DESCRIPTION
From the parking area (0.0 mi.) cross **Rockwell Road** and enter the woods to the west. The trail contours along the western slope of Rounds' Rock, heading south. After about three-quarters of a mile a short spur connects to the **Rounds' Rock Trail**. The Northrup Trail continues south to meet up again with Rockwell Road at 3.0 miles. Return the same way or be picked up at the road.

JONES' NOSE TRAIL

Distances: 0.5 mile to CCC Dynamite Trail, 1.0 mile to AT.
Estimated time: 25 minutes to CCC Dynamite Trail.
Blazes: Blue.
Map location: I – 6.
Maintenance: Department of Environmental Management.

Named for a farmer centuries ago, Jones' Nose offers fine views south and west into Connecticut and New York beyond Berkshire County. A short trail climbs through a clearing and then connects to the CCC Dynamite Trail and Appalachian Trail.

HOW TO GET THERE

- Refer to directions for Rockwell Road.
- Drive past the visitor center, into the park, past Rounds' Rock to the Jones' Nose Trailhead (19.9 mi.).

DESCRIPTION

From the parking area (0.0 mi.), hike north up the slope of Jones' Nose. After a quarter mile of views you enter the forest and continue to climb gradually towards Saddle Ball Mountain. At 0.5 mi. the **CCC Dynamite Trail** branches off to the left (north). There are good views west to the **Taconic Range** at 0.7 miles. You reach the **Appalachian Trail** at 1.0 mi. on the ridge of Saddle Ball Mountain.

CCC DYNAMITE TRAIL

Distance: 1.5 miles.
Estimated time: 50 minutes.
Blazes: Blue.
Map location: I – 7.
Maintenance: Department of Environmental Management.

Boy Scouts built this trail in 1990 and named it for the explosives the Civilian Conservation Corps stored in the area for construction of roads and trails in the 1930s. In spring and early summer this relatively flat trail is a favorite for viewing ferns and wildflowers.

HOW TO GET THERE:

- Refer to the Jones' Nose Trail description; the CCC Dynamite Trail starts at Jones' Nose.

DESCRIPTION

From the **Jones' Nose Trail** (0.0 mi.), bear left (north) at the signed junction for the CCC Dynamite Trail. You will hike nearly due north on a course along the western flank of Saddle Ball Mountain. If you look carefully, you may see the remains of crates used to store explosives decades ago.

At 1.5 mi. you reach **Rockwell Road**. **Sperry Road** continues north to a campground and a number of trails, including the **Hopper Trail** to the summit of Mt. Greylock.

GREYLOCK ROAD

Distance: 3.5 miles (approximately).
Estimated time: 10 minutes driving.
Blazes: None.
Map location: F – 8.
Maintenance: Town of New Ashford.

Many roads used to climb the slopes of Greylock from all sides. Notch and Rockwell Roads are the primary routes into the Reservation and to the summit. Greylock Road offers a secondary access from Route 7. This steep, dirt road is a fine, stout bike route as well.

HOW TO GET THERE
- Take Route 7 south toward Pittsfield from Williamstown.
- At 8.7 mi. turn left (east) beyond Roys Road at either of two entrances.

DESCRIPTION
After a ninety-degree left turn Greylock Road heads east on a steady grade and crosses the headwaters of East Branch of the Green River near the junction with old Bowers Road. Soon after, a gate marks the Mt. Greylock State Reservation Boundary. A northward, contouring climb brings you to **Rockwell Road** about 3.5 mi. from Route 7. Please drive slowly, the road is narrow and loose in places.

APPALACHIAN TRAIL
MT. GREYLOCK FROM CHESHIRE

Distance: 6.8 miles to Greylock Summit.
Estimated time: 4.5 hours.
Map location: L – 4.
Blazes: White.
Maintenance: Department of Environmental Management and Appalachian Mountain Club

Although many use the Appalachian Trail (AT) for long distance backpacking, it also provides excellent day hiking opportunities in the area. This section of the AT is the principal southern access to the Greylock Range. Along the way are a number of historic coach roads as well as the upgraded automobile roads of today.

HOW TO GET THERE
- From the junction of Routes 2 and 7, take Route 2 east to the junction with Route 8 in North Adams (5.1 mi.).
- Go south on Route 8.
- At 15.4 mi., turn right on West Mountain Road.
- Follow West Mountain Road to Outlook Avenue and turn right (15.7 mi.).
- Drive 0.8 mi. to the Appalachian Trail trailhead junction. Look for white rectangular blazes on left and right sides of the road.

DESCRIPTION
From Outlook Avenue (0.0 mi.), head west, skirting the southern edge of an open field and cross an old stone wall on the north side of an adjacent field. Ascend gently into the woods to gradually steeper terrain until you reach a height of land.

Here the trail levels out and runs parallel to the ridgeline. You pass a small swampy area and cross several streams before climbing to a high plateau. A gradual descent brings you to a red spruce grove and a junction with **Old Adams Road** 150 feet west of its intersection with the **Redgate Road** (2.7 mi.).

From the spruce grove, you weave between huge boulders and at one point pass through one that is split into two pieces. As the trail ascends the southeast shoulder of Saddle Ball Mountain, the grade quickly becomes steeper.

A short path to the left leads 30 feet to an overlook (3.0 mi.) into Kitchen Brook Valley to the south. Be cautious when approaching the overlook, as it is very steep, with a sharp drop off.

Just past the overlook, a second side trail to the right leads to a brook, Mark Noepel Shelter and a camping area. The shelter is quite large, with bunks and a loft. Two tent platforms and 2-3 tent sites are also available.

Across an old logging road, the AT ascends a ridge covered by balsam fir with good views to the right on a 200-foot side trail (4.1 mi.). On top of Saddle Ball Mountain, you reach the junction with an older section of the AT (4.2 mi.). This is now the **Jones' Nose Trail** to views of the Catskill Mountains (0.3 mi.), and the Jones' Nose parking lot on **Rockwell Road** (1.0 mi.). The current route veers east, bypassing a large swamp and crossing two intermittent brooks (5.0 mi.).

As the trail emerges from a sphagnum moss bog, you meet the topmost switchback in Rockwell Road (5.9 mi.). Cut back into the woods on the right. As you cross the road a second time (6.2 mi.), you intersect both the **Cheshire Harbor Trail** and the **Hopper Trail**.

The AT continues to a wood road and a small reservoir, where it loops east to cross Rockwell and **Notch Roads** (6.4 mi.). To reach the summit of Mt. Greylock (6.8 mi.), follow the former Misery Trail, passing a TV tower before the **Bascom Lodge**. From the memorial tower at the summit, the Catskills, Adirondacks, Green Mountains and Berkshires are visible on a clear day.

HIKING IN THE NORTHEAST

The North Berkshire area is wonderfully accessible and filled with endless nooks and crannies to explore. However, there are other areas to explore farther away with the help of transportation.

Nearby, Central and South Berkshire County have numerous pleasant walks and hikes. Refer to *Hikes and Walks in Berkshire County* or *A Guide to Natural Places in Berkshire County* for more information. To explore other parts of Massachusetts, including the Hoosac Range and Route 2 corridor directly east of Williamstown, check out the *AMC Massachussetts and Rhode Island Trail Guide*.

North along Route 7 the Green Mountains of Vermont stretch over 200 miles to Canada. The *Long Trail Guide* and *Day Hikes in Vermont* published by the Green Mountain Club describe the hundreds of trails available.

Only three hours away, the Adirondack Mountains of upstate New York draw visitors to the mountains and rivers of the six million acre Adirondack State Park. The Adirondack Mountain Club publishes a series of guides, each one devoted to a region of the park.

Farther east, the highest peaks of New England are found in the White Mountains of New Hampshire. Alpine terrain, glacial valleys, waterfalls, the Appalachian Mountain Club (AMC) huts and an extensive trail network attract hikers to the area. The AMC publishes the *White Mountain Guide*, now in its 26th edition.

Stretching from Georgia to Maine, the Appalachian Trail passes through southern New York, Connecticut, Massachusetts, Vermont and New Hampshire. The Appalachian Trail Conference publishes a guide series if you wish to follow part or all of this famous path.

Mt. Katahdin in Maine's Baxter State Park is a mecca for many New England hikers as the northern terminus of the Appalachian Trail. Another attraction in Maine is Cadillac Mountain in Acadia National Park; on some days of the year, it is the first point in the continental United States that sunlight hits directly.

Refer to the bibliography for more complete information on the references mentioned above.

WINTER

With the falling of the leaves, the masks of green are stripped off the hillsides, revealing the diversity and uniqueness of each ridge and valley, rock and stream, old shed or oil well hitherto unseen. It is in the winter, when the hills bear their innermost selves, that we get to know them. Then, in the spring...we can look at the hills as old friends few others understand.

John W. Walker

Winter weather...some find it intimidating, others find it challenging. Some consider it just plain fun. Whether you are planning a short morning ski through the forest on a chilly day, a midnight adventure up Pine Cobble in the storm of the century, or a backpacking trip on a rainy summer day, cold weather presents its own threats and rewards.

This section outlines some things to keep in mind when planning a trip, at any time when you may encounter cold weather. Although they are generalized as winter safety, be aware that wind and rain on the summit of Mt. Greylock can make an August day more dangerous than a cold clear day in February. With some preparation and common sense, however, both can be fun.

SHORTER DAYS

We all know that winter means shorter days, but we don't always take that into consideration when planning trips. Be sure to carry headlamps, get an early start, and remember that the pace at which you travel may be significantly slower than it is at other times of year. While three miles per hour might be realistic during the summer, snow and ice may reduce this to less than one mile per hour. When the snow is deep and finding a route becomes a challenge, covering a mile may take even more time.

DEHYDRATION

Hypothermia and frostbite are the most obvious cold related problems, but they are not the only ones. Dehydration, which "thickens" your blood and decreases its rate of flow, can cause headaches, exhaustion, and an increased susceptibility to frostbite. The cold dry winter air removes more moisture with each breath and the cold decreases your thirst response as well.

Drink all the time, whether or not you are thirsty. You should drink at least two quarts on a day hike, and 5-6 quarts a day if you are winter camping. For extended camping trips, pack herbal teas instead of coffee or hot cocoa. The caffeine in these drinks can exacerbate dehydration.

NUTRITION

Exposure to cold air constantly drains heat away from your body, so you need a large number of calories just to stay warm. While most people probably won't need to eat sticks of butter, as some mountaineers do, you will need to allow even more food than you would for normal outdoor activity (up to 4,000-6,000 calories per person per day).

To add to the challenge, cold will make consuming your food harder. For example, you might have to break your candy bar into bite-size pieces with an ice ax! In preparation, put your trail snacks in an inner pocket to keep them warm. Also, fill your water bottle with hot water and stick it in a pair of socks for insulation. Ice forms at the top of water, so store the bottle upside-down...just make sure it doesn't leak.

COLD

An obvious challenge of winter recreation is the ever present cold that brings us ice and snow. An even more obvious antidote is heat, which we need to generate and retain through movement and insulation. Stay active in the cold and as long as you eat and drink enough (see above) your body can generate plenty of heat. With proper clothing (see What to Wear) you can capture that precious heat and stay dry along the way.

Cold Weather Tips
- Keep your torso and legs warm to avoid cold hands and feet.
- Always wear a hat.
- At rest breaks you may have to walk around or jump up and down to generate heat.
- Wear a sock and boot combination with enough room to wiggle your toes.
- In the wind, be sure to wear a shell, otherwise all your heat gets swept away.
- For cold hands and feet swing your arms or legs to force blood to the extremities.
- If camping, exercise before you get into your sleeping bag in order to go to sleep warm.
- Keep a positive, happy attitude and think warm!

ICE AND SNOW

Even if the snow at the base of a mountain is well packed or shallow, don't rely on either of these being true as you gain altitude. A few feet of powder can become a tiring obstacle, so carry skis or snowshoes if you are likely to be traveling on unbroken trails. If you intend to hike above treeline, or to try some technical climbing in winter, evaluate your skill level carefully. Go with more experienced people or hire a guide if necessary.

As is true for all activities, there are dangers associated with winter sports. The majority of these, however, are simply due to poor preparation and bad decisions. If you travel in groups and stay dry, fed, and well-hydrated, winter activities can provide some of your most wonderful moments outside. Despite all of the potential problems, breaking trail through fresh powder, climbing a frozen waterfall, or battling against high winds on an icy ridge can be both exhilarating and rewarding.

WINTER ACTIVITIES

Snow and ice provide an opportunity for different modes of travel in the North Berkshire Hills. Unfortunately, the vagaries of weather may deny you snow when you most want it, but usually there are at least a few weeks of cover in a winter. When the snow is shallow or firm hiking is the best way to go on local trails. But when deeper snows slow you down, snowshoeing and skiing are fun ways to explore. Snowmaking keeps the downhill ski areas in shape from Christmas into spring. For those who like ice, crampons and ice axes can take you on icy mountain ridges or up frozen waterfalls.

SNOWSHOEING

The advent of modern aluminum and plastic snowshoes has fueled an explosion of snowshoeing across the country. A simple concept, the surface area of a snowshoe keeps you from sinking and reduces the fatigue of "postholing" with each step. You do not need special boots. Any warm comfortable ones will do. All trails in this guide may be snowshoed, especially the steeper or more narrow trails that may be difficult to ski. With some basic navigation skills you can explore freely off the trails since snow minimizes your impact. The WOC Equipment Room has many pairs of snowshoes for use by members of the Outing Club.

CROSS COUNTRY SKIING

Rather than the adrenaline rush of zooming down a mountain on downhill skis, cross country (nordic) skiing offers the peaceful serenity of snow-covered woods. It is one of the best forms of cardiovascular exercise, since it involves all major muscle groups and is easier on the joints than running or even walking.

Cross country skiing in this guide refers to groomed terrain or lower-elevation, valley routes close to population centers. The more challenging and remote terrain of the mountains above is classified as Backcountry Skiing and described separately.

Nordic skiing is also one of the most environmentally friendly of outdoor sports, because snow cushions the trails from any significant impact. Safety is less of an issue when cross-country skiing, but you should listen for snowmobiles that could be in the area. Falling is common enough and can be fun, especially if you use the favorite sit-down crash method. Sometimes steep hills are tricky, but as long as you control your speed and keep your poles pointed behind you (so that they don't stab you when crashing) the impact is usually cushioned by snow.

WOC members may use the nordic ski equipment available in the Equipment Room. During Winter Study WOC offers cross-country classes and transportation to local trails. For more information refer to Lauren Stevens' *Skiing in the Berkshire Hills*.

Taconic Golf Course

The golf course is located on the south side of Weston Field, on the edge of the Williams campus. Gentle slopes and open terrain make this a great area for the first-time skier.

Stone Hill

A beautiful place to ski, although there are some steeper sections above the Clark Art Institute. Zigzag up a steep hill so your skis can grip on a more gradual angle. Refer to the trail descriptions or simply explore the pastures.

Hopkins Forest

As of January 1999 the Loop Trail will have tracks set when there is adequate snow. Hopkins Forest is a good place to try some steeper terrain, especially on the upper loop. Use the trail description in this guide.

Field Farm

This flat land managed by The Trustees of Reservations has 4.5 miles of trail along forest, field, marsh and pond. Refer to the description in the Taconic Range section of this guide.

Greylock Glen

A network of trails used extensively by snowmobiles above the town of Adams. There are some skier-only trails.

CROSS COUNTRY SKI AREAS

Always call ahead to check if the following areas have enough snow to open. You can also check their websites or look for other Berkshire cross-country areas at http://www.berkshireweb.com

Brodie Mountain Ski Touring Center, New Ashford.
(413) 443-4752
http://www.skibrodie.com

Mount Greylock Ski Club, Williamstown.
A small downhill and cross country area in Goodell Hollow along Roaring Brook on the west side of Mt. Greylock.
(413) 445-7887

Prospect Mountain, Woodford, Vermont.
With a base at 2,250 feet, Prospect has the most reliable skiing in the area. A 30+ kilometer network of groomed trails offers great cross country skiing and skating in the Green Mountains, 35 minutes from Williamstown. From Prospect you can access great backcountry skiing in the Green Mountains.
(802) 242-2575
http://users.aol.com/xcski/private/HomePage.html

BACKCOUNTRY SKIING

The Williamstown area offers almost unlimited opportunities for backcountry skiing expeditions. Once you have learned basic cross-country skiing techniques, cold weather travel and navigation, you are ready to journey up into the hills. Blazed trails are a logical place to start, but feel free to explore throughout the hills as your skills and knowledge increase. Reread the Starting Out section and Winter Sports introduction for a few preparation and safety reminders.

The ski equipment you use on flat or groomed trails can be used on more challenging terrain, but eventually you will want to investigate heavier equipment and telemark skiing. Telemark skiing uses stiffer boots, wider skis with metal edges and sturdy free-heel binding systems to negotiate backcountry terrain.

Below is a list of local trails well suited to skiing, with a few notes for each. Other trails are steep or narrow and must be ascended by switchbacking through the forest or on telemark skis with skins for uphill traction. Refer to the hiking trail descriptions for specific directions.

Green Mountain

Dome Trail .... Watch for snowmobiles. The top part may be difficult to follow.

Taconic Range

Hopkins Forest .... See Cross Country, above.

Birch Brook Trail .... Good loop with R.R.R. Brooks trail.

Fitch Trail .... Somewhat steep up Bee Hill, advanced.

R.R.R. Brooks Trail .... Beautiful gradual climb to the Taconic Crest. Lower section may be treacherous with little or icy snow.

Shepherd's Well Trail ...... Completes R.R.R. Brooks Trail to crest, combine with Birch Brook Trail and Taconic Crest Trail.

WRLF Loop Trail .... A flat logging grade makes for a short, gentle ski.

Berlin Pass Trail .... Sustained climb, good access for downhill runs at the Old Williams College Ski area.

Old Williams Ski Area ..... A fun steep descent from Berlin Mountain for advanced skiers.

Field Farm .... See Cross Country, above.

Taconic Crest Trail .... High and often windy with many snowmobiles.

Old Petersburg Ski Area .. Abandoned and partially overgrown downhill ski trails south of Petersburg Pass.

Greylock Range

Money Brook Trail .... After second bridge, take cut-off south to the Hopper Trail to return to the trailhead.

Roaring Brook Trail .... Consistently demanding climb, advanced. Descend Stony Ledge Trail.

Stony Ledge Trail .... Originally cut as a downhill trail, advanced skiers (see below).

Notch Road .... Steep road with snowmobile traffic.

Bellows Pipe Trail .... To summit of Greylock, steepest at top.

Old Summit Road .... Bypasses Notch Road near Mt. Williams.

Cheshire Harbor Trail ...... Popular route up Greylock with snowmobile traffic.

Old Adams Road .... Snowmobiles.

Thunderbolt Trail .... THE ski descent of the area. For experienced backcountry or downhill skiers (see below).

Redgate Road .... Snowmobiles.

Silverfox Trail .... Snowmobiles.

Rockwell Road .... Heavy snowmobile traffic.

Brook and Berry Trails .... Short loops near Mount Greylock Visitor Center.

Northrup Trail .... Alternative to Rockwell Road.

CCC Dynamite Trail .... Alternative to Rockwell Road.

Sperry Road .... Part of the Roaring Brook – Stony Ledge loop.

Note: When skiing anywhere in the Mt. Greylock Reservation, be aware that the Department of Environmental Management may change the trail uses from time to time; i.e. snowmobiles only or skiing only. It is your responsibility to find out what the current usage regulations are, and to obey them.

BACKCOUNTRY SKI DESCENTS

A few trails in the area were cut specifically for downhill skiing during the 1930's through the 1950's. These are challenging runs for advanced backcountry or downhill skiers.

THUNDERBOLT SKI TRAIL

Distance: 1.6 miles.
Vertical drop: 2,175 feet.
Map location: N – 10.

This exceptionally fast and difficult trail descends the east slope of Mt. Greylock from the summit to Thiel Farm, west of Adams. The breathtaking descent earned its name from a rollercoaster at Revere Beach, an amusement park outside Boston. In 1938, it was the site of the Eastern Downhill Championships, which attracted a crowd of 6,000 people. Under favorable conditions, such as deep powder or heavy spring snow, it can be an exciting experience for the advanced skier. Refer to the hiking trail description.

STONY LEDGE SKI TRAIL

Distance: 2.1 miles.
Vertical drop: 1,400 feet.
Map location: H – 10.

Like the Thunderbolt, the Civilian Conservation Corps constructed this trail with the Mount Greylock Ski Club for downhill skiers. The trail has not been maintained for skiing so brush may be a problem except with a couple feet of snow. This steep and challenging trail descends from Stony Ledge at the end of Sperry Road to Goodell Hollow in South Williamstown. Ascend the more gradual, though still challenging, Roaring Brook Trail to make a loop. Refer to the hiking trail description.

DOWNHILL SKI AREAS

If you want to improve your skiing skills or avoid the uphill climb of free heel skiing, you can head to one of the many downhill ski areas within an hour of Williamstown.

North Berkshire
 Brodie. New Ashford ....(413) 443-4752
 Jiminy Peak, Hancock ....(413) 738-5500

Central and South Berkshire
 Bousquet, Pittsfield ....(413) 442-8316
 Butternut, Great Barrington ....(413) 528-2000
 Catamount, South Egremont ....(413) 528-1262
 Otis Ridge, Otis ....(413) 269-4444

Southern Vermont
 Bromley, Manchester Center ....(802) 824-5522
 Mount Snow, Dover & Wilmington ....(802) 464-3333
 Stratton Mountain, Stratton ....(802) 297-2200

ICE CLIMBING

Modern waterfall ice climbing has evolved from mountaineering during the 20th century. New England winters often produce prodigious amounts of ice on crags throughout the mountains from the Berkshires to Canada.

The sport relies heavily on specialized equipment including stiff boots, crampons, ice axes, helmets, warm clothes, a climbing rope and anchor hardware. You also need specific knowledge to safely climb ice, a fickle material.

If ice climbing interests you, contact the Williams Outing Club or a guide service to get an introduction to this fun and challenging sport.

BIKING

A bike ride provides an excellent opportunity for adventure and exploration in the Williamstown area, bringing you into closer contact with some of the gorgeous scenery that surrounds us. Whether on trails or local roads, the riding in and around Williamstown is superb, with possibilities for anything from easy beginner excursions to extreme expert rides.

To ensure fun and successful rides, all cyclists should follow a few basic safety guidelines. Wear a helmet to protect your head and glasses to shield your eyes from sand, mud and sticks. Gloves are not absolutely necessary, but they will protect your hands if you crash. Perhaps the best way to prevent a serious problem when riding is always to stay within your ability and comfort level, as accidents usually happen when you get tired and begin to make mistakes. On the same note, always ride with another person, so that there will be someone around to help you if you do have an accident or get lost.

No matter what kind of bike you have, be sure to keep it in good condition. Clean it on a regular basis, and take it to a local bike shop for periodic tune-ups. Before each ride, check to see that the brakes are working, and that the seat height is properly adjusted (your knee should be slightly bent when at the bottom of the pedal stroke). Always carry a patch kit, a pump, water (one bottle per hour) and change or a calling card number. If you are going out for more than a few hours, you should also consider bringing some food, extra tools and warm clothes.

MOUNTAIN BIKING

In recent years, mountain biking has become an extremely popular pastime in the Williamstown area, offering gorgeous scenery without the traffic that can be a problem for bikers on the road. Possibilities for exploration include miles of old logging roads and some hiking trails. Because of the large number of people who enjoy mountain biking, it is important that riders do their best to minimize their impact.

This means not riding when the trails are extremely wet (especially in the springtime) and not skidding by locking up your brakes. Respect posted signs indicating trail restrictions and do not ride on trails which are marked "Hiking only." Always respect the rights of private land owners, and ask for permission before riding on their land. If you are unsure about the status of a trail, check with the Outing Club or local bike shop.

While you are on the trail, it is important to respect the other trail users, including all terrain vehicles (ATV's), hikers, and horses. Slow down or dismount when you are approaching hikers or horseback riders, and let them know that you are behind them. When you see or hear an ATV approaching be sure to get out of the way. Remember that our relationship with the other trail users determines future access to our favorite trails!

If you are new to mountain biking, try riding some local roads first and then move on to trails. Join a Williams Outing Club or Mountain Goat ride to get an introduction to the area. A lot of rides in the area have significant elevation gain, so be ready. Thankfully, what goes up, must come down!

DIRT ROADS

Many roads change from pavement to dirt away from the commercial and more populated areas. These dirt roads often access double track roads or trails even further away. Refer to the map and location grid to find these roads, and link them together to form longer rides, explore!

Northwest Hill Road
Map location: G – 20.
This well-maintained dirt road passes open fields, a great look at the Taconic and Greylock Ranges and some classic wooded areas. Follow directions to **Hopkins Forest Loop Trail** and ride past the entrance to Hopkins Forest.

Petersburg Road
Map location: F – 19.
An old route over the Taconic Range that starts on the pavement of West Main St. (starts at Williams Inn) and turns to dirt on Petersburg Road. Just before the last house bear left by a gate and through a field to an eroded double track heading south to Route 2 (Old Petersburg Road).

Bee Hill Road
Map location: G – 18.
A steep climb from Route 7 to the south of town with amazing views of Stone Hill, the Hopper and Greylock. An abandoned extension across Route 2 links up with Berlin Mountain Road. To get there, ride south on Routes 2 and 7 from Field Park. Bee Hill Road is the second road to the right after crossing Hemlock Brook.

Berlin Mountain Road
Map location: E – 17.
Part of the original Boston - Albany post road and access to the **Old Williams College Ski Area** and **Berlin Pass Trail**. Refer to directions for the Berlin Pass Trail or access it from Bee Hill Road and the abandoned Bee Hill Road extension across Route 2 .

White Oaks Road
Map location: I – 21.
This road turns to dirt in Vermont near the **Broad Brook** and **Dome Trails**. As the labyrinth of eroded road grades in the area are on private land, please respect postings and landowners.

Mason Hill Road
  Map location: H – 22.
  From Route 7 in Pownal, Vermont, Mason Hill Road climbs steeply above the Hoosic River Valley to a fantastic view of the Taconic Range.

County Road
  Map location: K – 27.
  A several hour, challenging ride from Pownal Center to Stamford, Vermont. Not dry and rideable until late spring. Make sure you are in good shape and leave enough time before dark.

TRAILS

Many trails in the North Berkshire area are open to Mountain Biking, others are definitely closed and some are specifically posted. Please respect official trail restrictions to protect bike access in the future and when status is uncertain try to contact a landowner or public land agency before you ride.

For directions, refer to the hiking trail descriptions by using the index. Remember that the estimated times in the descriptions are for hiking, not biking. Below is a list of trails definitely open to mountain bikes, consider all others described in this guide closed unless you see a posting specifically open to bikes.

Stone Hill
  Pasture Loop .... Closed in woods, pasture open.
  Stone Hill Road .... Open, make part of a loop.

Green Mountain
  Dome Trail .... Open lower half.

Taconic Range
  Berlin Pass Trail .... Open, gullied and rocky.
  Old Ski Area .... Open but steep.
  Phelps Trail .... Open, steep in places.
  Mills Hollow Trail .... Open, road grade to Crest.

Bentley Hollow Trail .... Open but very rocky.
Taconic Crest Trail .... Open south of Route 2. Closed in Hopkins Forest to the north.

Note: Bikes are strictly prohibited on all trails in Hopkins Forest due to ongoing research.

Greylock Range
Stony Ledge Trail .... Open, steep downhill.
Greylock Road .... Open, dirt road up Greylock.
Notch Road .... Open, steep paved road.
Bellows Pipe Trail .... Open, steep at top.
Bellows Pipe Extension ... Open, to Gould Farm.
Cheshire Harbor Trail ...... Open, popular route.
Old Adams Road .... Open, access from Cheshire Harbor Trail.
Redgate Road .... Open, Greylock Glen to Rockwell Road.
Silverfox Trail .... Open, east side.
Greylock Glen .... Open in some areas.
Rockwell Road .... Open, gradual paved road.
Sperry Road .... Open, flat road to Stony Ledge.

ROAD BIKING

There are a number of easily accessible and beautiful loops in the Williamstown area, ranging in length from ten miles to over seventy. Some are virtually flat, while others include one or more steep and challenging climbs. A small selection of possible rides is described below. Refer to the *WOC Bicycling Guide and Map* (available in local stores) or *Bike Rides in the Berkshire Hills* for more routes. You can always use the *North Berkshire Trails* map to plan your own loops. For areas farther away consult maps available from WOC, the Mountain Goat, or the Spoke.

When you ride on the road, do not forget that you are a vehicle. You need to make yourself as visible as you can to cars that may not be able to see you very well. Wear bright colors, and make sure that your bike is equipped with lights and reflectors. Obey all traffic rules and regulations, and know the appropriate hand signals to make when you are turning or stopping.

The routes are listed in order of length from shortest to longest.

FIVE CORNERS

Distance: 9.8 miles.
Estimated time: 45 minutes to 1 hour.
Elevation change: Minimal.

Very popular with runners as well as with cyclists, the combination of gentle terrain and relatively short distance make this a pleasant introductory ride. There is one moderate uphill directly north of Five Corners, but after that it is downhill until Williamstown!

DESCRIPTION

Ride east on Route 2, past the Williamstown Savings Bank. Turn right onto Water Street (Route 43) and follow it to "Five Corners," the intersection of Routes 7 and 43 in South Williamstown (5.0 mi.). Turn right onto Route 7 and return to Williamstown. Or turn around and return the way you came for a gradual downhill.

NORTHWEST HILL ROAD

Distance: 11.3 miles.
Estimated time: 1 hour.
Elevation gain: Minimal.

This relatively well-maintained dirt road offers lots of open fields, a great look at the Taconic Mountains, and some classic wooded areas.

DESCRIPTION

From Field Park, take Route 7 north to Bulkley Street (0.4 mi.). Turn left on Bulkley Street; continue across the bridge and up the hill to the T-intersection with Northwest Hill Road (1.2 mi.). Turn right onto Northwest Hill Road, and follow it until you reach Route 346 (6.1 mi.). Take a right on Route 346 and follow it south to Route 7 and continue to Williamstown.

LUCE ROAD – RESERVOIR ROAD

Distance: 12.7 miles.
Estimated time: 1.5 hours.
Elevation Change: 700 feet.

Although the road near the reservoir tends to be a bit rough, this route provides a good alternative to Route 2 when your destination is somewhere south of North Adams. Near the reservoir there is a very good view of the Purple Valley, along with a close-up look at Mt. Prospect.

DESCRIPTION

Ride east on Route 2 to Luce Road and turn right (1.5 mi.). Ride uphill a couple miles toward Mt. Prospect, past the reservoirs, and bear right onto Notch Road. Follow Notch Road to a junction with Reservoir Road (5.3 mi.). From here, turn left (downhill) onto Reservoir Road and continue to North Adams and the intersection with Route 8 (7.9 mi.). Go left onto Route 8 and follow the road signs to Route 2. Turn left to follow Route 2 west back to Williamstown.

POWNAL CENTER LOOP

Distance: 16.8 miles.
Estimated time: 1 to 2 hours.
Elevation change: about 400 feet.

One of the nicest short loops around, this ride has fine views and some moderate hills. The road from Pownal Center to North Pownal is second only to Greylock in downhill fun and excitement.

DESCRIPTION
From Field Park, follow Route 7 north out of Williamstown. Continue along Route 7 up the hill that begins at the Green Mountain Park. At Pownal Center (7.8 mi.), take a left on North Pownal Road and coast downhill. In North Pownal, turn left onto Route 346 (9.7 mi.). Route 346 leads back to Route 7 (11.8 mi.), turn right (downhill) to return to Williamstown.

RIVER ROAD – MIDDLE/CROSS ROADS

Distance: 17.0 miles Cross Road, 20.2 miles Middle Road.
Estimated time: 2 hours.
Elevation Change: 400 feet.

This route provides a useful alternative to Route 2 when your destination is somewhere north of North Adams. Middle and Cross Roads are also worth riding in their own right. Both are enjoyable, quiet rides on a plateau to the north of North Adams. The ascent to the plateau is a shockingly steep, but mercifully short, hill.

DESCRIPTION
Ride east on Route 2 and take a left on Cole Avenue. At the end of Cole Avenue, turn right onto North Hoosac Road and follow it to North Adams, where it emerges one block north of Route 2. Follow Route 2 for a short distance until Route 8 branches to the left (6.9 mi.). Take either of the two lefts within the next few miles. The first is Cross Road (8.4 mi.), and the second is Middle Road (10.2 mi.). Both lead back to North Adams at River Street .

ROUTE 43 – BRODIE MOUNTAIN ROAD

Distance: 28.8 miles.
Riding Time: 2 to 3 hours.
Elevation Change: 900 feet.

The enjoyable rolling terrain along Route 43 could well have been designed specifically for biking. Brodie Mountain Road is a good early-season introduction to a moderate hill climb. Beware of the heavy traffic on the final leg of this loop.

DESCRIPTION

Ride east on Route 2 to the intersection of Routes 2 and 43 (Water Street) and turn right. Stay on Route 43 through the intersection with Route 7 and turn left on Brodie Mountain Road, marked "Jiminy Peak Ski Area" (13.8 mi.). This road climbs a moderate hill and ends on a sharp downhill corner at Route 7 (16.4 mi.), be careful. Return to Williamstown via Route 7 or in combination with Route 43.

PETERSBURG PASS

Distance: 28.8 miles.
Estimated time: 2 to 3 hours.
Elevation change: 1,400 feet.

Although Petersburg Pass is not incredibly steep, and in fact gets easier after the first half mile, it is the longest climb in any of these rides besides Mt. Greylock. The connection with Route 346 makes for an enjoyable and, after the Pass, a very relaxing ride.

DESCRIPTION

Take Routes 2 and 7 south until Route 2 branches right (2.8 mi.). Follow Route 2 up and over Petersburg Pass to its intersection with Route 22. Take Route 22 north to Route 346 (16.2 mi.), then turn right on Route 346 and return to Route 7 (23.8 mi.).

BENNINGTON – ROUTE 22 – ROUTE 346

Distance: 42.6 miles.
Estimated time: 3 to 4 hours.
Elevation change: 400 feet up Pownal hill, minimal thereafter.

This nice, long ride avoids traffic most of the way, except for a short time in Bennington. At Barber's Pond, on a back road to Bennington, there is a beautiful cross-section of an esker, a sinuous ridge formed by glacial activity.

DESCRIPTION

Start riding north on Route 7, and follow it uphill after the Green Mountain Park. At the crest of the hill in Pownal Center, take the only right (7.8 mi.) onto South Stream Road. As you approach Bennington you will encounter some forks; follow the roads that retain the double yellow lines and you should end up on Beech Street. At the Beech Street intersection with Route 9 (17.0 mi.) turn left onto Route 9. Follow signs through Bennington to Route 22 (26.5 mi.), then turn left onto Route 22 south and continue to the intersection with Route 346 (29.0 mi.). Take a left on Route 346, return to Pownal and continue to Williamstown.

MT. GREYLOCK

Distance: 35.4 miles.
Estimated time: At least two to three hours.
Elevation Change: 2,800 feet.

This is unquestionably the steepest and most challenging ride in the Williamstown vicinity. Euphemistically, cyclists often call this an "extremely rewarding" ride. After entering the Mount Greylock Reservation, you ascend almost 3000 feet in 6.7 miles.

Despite the difficulties, this ride is breathtakingly beautiful, with stunning views from many points on the way to the summit, as well as from the summit itself. Vehicle traffic on both Notch and Rockwell Roads can be quite heavy, particularly in the summer, so keep to one side of the road and stay alert.

DESCRIPTION

Ride east on Route 2, take a right on Luce Road (1.5 mi.) and bear left as it becomes Pattison Road. Just past the reservoir, bear right onto Notch Road and continue to the Mount Greylock State Reservation (5.3 mi.). From the entrance, climb steeply to the intersection of Notch and Rockwell Roads (11.3 mi.), and take Rockwell Road to the summit (12.0 mi.).

After you are finished catching your breath and admiring the view, follow Rockwell Road down the south side of the mountain. The road descends first steeply and then more gradually to intersect Route 7 just north of Lanesboro (20.4 mi.). To complete the loop, ride north on Route 7 to Williamstown (35.4 mi.).

FLY-FISHING

A ll streams are talkative, and a hill stream is the greatest
chatterer of all. It is never boring, yet always soothing.
It is a thousand voices in one, and one voice in a thousand.
Do not think as you lie beside it, but let it think for you. Then
you will hear the voice and message of the hill.

Frank Smythe

Williamstown and the surrounding areas offer some of the most
productive fly-fishing in Massachusetts. The Green River, Hoosic
River and smaller tributaries flow through town, and the Deerfield
River is only a short drive away. These waterways have many
accesses for excellent fishing in all but the coldest months of the
year. Brown, rainbow, and brook trout inhabit these waters; in the
future salmon may be introduced into the Deerfield River.

Several fishing accesses are marked with a fish icon on the *North
Berkshire Trails* map. Many of these are protected by the Massachusetts Division of Fisheries and Wildlife.

EQUIPMENT

Before purchasing a fishing rod or any other equipment, you should
talk to an experienced friend or salesperson. There are many excellent books about tackle and fishing paraphernalia. If you would
like to gain some experience before buying your own equipment,
contact the Williams Outing Club for more information about fishing trips in the local area. WOC members may use club equipment if they possess a current fishing license..

LICENSES

A fishing license must be purchased every year and displayed vis-
ibly when in the field. A license is only valid in the state where it
is purchased, so be careful about straying into Vermont from
Williamstown. Massachusetts licenses can be obtained at the

Williamstown Town Hall, located at 31 North Street (Route 7) just
north of Field Park.

CATCH-AND-RELEASE

Please practice catch-and-release fishing wherever you fish. Some
important guidelines to remember are:

- Use barbless hooks to facilitate releasing the fish and mini-
mize damage to the jaws.
- If you use a net, use a fine mesh to avoid damaging fins.
- Wet your hands before handling the fish.
- When removing a hook, keep the fish as close to the water
as possible.
- After removing the hook, place the fish gently in moving
water facing upstream.
- Keep a firm (but not too tight) hold on the fish until it is
strong enough to swim away.

Using these guidelines, you should be able to have a great time
without disturbing the fragile river ecosystem.

GREEN RIVER

The Green River holds many small brown, rainbow and brook trout
between six and thirteen inches in length; occasionally a lucky or
skilled person can catch one as long as fifteen inches. These fish
are very healthy and always put up a good fight. Spring and summer are the prime fishing times on the Green River because of the
abundant fly hatches.

During this period, a brown or rainbow trout may jump clear
out of the water for a fly that looks only remotely similar to a
natural fly. In general, the trout in the Green River are not very
selective, making the river a great one for the beginning angler.

HOW TO GET THERE

- The Green River runs parallel to Water Street (Route 43),
and can be fished almost anywhere you can park your car.
Please heed all "No Trespassing" signs and do not cross

private property unless you have the landowner's permission.
- One particularly accessible area is Mt. Hope Park, located 3 miles south of the intersection of Route 2 and Water Street.
- The Massachusetts Division of Fisheries and Wildlife maintains an access point at the entrance to Mt. Hope Farm, south of Mt. Hope Park along Route 43.

RECOMMENDED FLIES
- Elk Hair Caddis (size 12-16).
- March Brown (size 12-16).
- Adams (size 14-18).
- Hare's Ear Nymph (size 10-16).
- Pheasant Tail Nymph (size 14-16) for big fish.
- Muddler Minnow (any size) in bigger pools.

HOOSIC RIVER

As the water level on the Green River decreases during the hot summer months, the Hoosic River becomes a particularly attractive fishing spot. The Hoosic runs from Clarksburg through Cheshire, Adams and North Adams into Williamstown, before continuing into Vermont and finally into New York.

While not as easily accessible as the Green River, the Hoosic River holds some of the area's biggest brown and rainbow trout, ranging in size from fourteen to twenty-three inches. Since a fish rising is a rarity on the Hoosic, nymph and streamer fishing is most common.

Do not eat any of the Hoosic River trout, as they contain high levels of Polychlorinated Biphenyls (PCBs) and heavy metals that are suspected of being highly carcinogenic. Please release all Hoosic River fish!

HOW TO GET THERE
- There are many access points along the Hoosic. Refer to the *North Berkshire Trails* map to find the trails, canoe access and fishing access points indicated.

RECOMMENDED FLIES
- Hare's Ear Nymph (size 12).
- Black Wooly Worm (size 6-10).
- Black Marabou Muddler (size 4-10).
- Other assorted dark streamers.

OTHER LOCAL BROOKS

Hemlock Brook and Broad Brook are two of the larger streams that empty into the Hoosic River. The Massachusetts Division of Fisheries and Wildlife maintains several posted access points to Hemlock Brook along Routes 2 and 7 south of Williamstown (see *North Berkshire Trails* map).

Broad Brook is a breathtakingly beautiful stream choked with cobbles in White Oaks, north of Williamstown. Respect private property in the area and be conscious of the Vermont border near the Broad Brook trailhead (see map).

DEERFIELD RIVER

The Deerfield offers some of the best trout fishing in the entire northeast, in some of the most beautiful surroundings. It has a large population of both stocked and native brown, rainbow, and brook trout. There are also plans to introduce salmon into the river at some point in the future. During the spring and summer, the Deerfield offers great dry-fly fishing. It is particularly famous for its Caddis hatches.

Water levels may rise without warning for hydroelectric power generation, so always inquire about water release schedules before venturing to the river. Call the New England Power Company at (413) 625–8414 for water release times. A water level of 75-150 cubic feet per second is ideal for fishing, but levels of 700 CFS and above can be dangerous.

For more information on fishing the Deerfield refer to *The Deerfield River Guidebook*.

HOW TO GET THERE

- From the junction of Routes 2 and 7, take Route 2 east towards North Adams.

- Follow Route 2 past North Adams up and over the famous "hairpin." Turn at first left after the bronzed elk historical marker onto Whitcomb Hill Road at 12.6 miles.

- Follow the steep winding Whitcomb Hill Road all the way to the end, turn left onto River Road heading towards Monroe.

- Follow River Road for 2.0 mi., bear right onto a road directing you to a catch-and-release fishing area. Park along the shoulder or at designated parking near out houses. Look for trails leading a short walk to the put-in.

- This mile long stretch is the best area for fishing, but all fish must be handled very carefully and returned unharmed to the river.

- You can also take a right at the stop sign and drive five miles down river to the ZOAR campground, where parking is available for easy river access. This, however, is not a catch-and-release section; canoes and kayaks may interrupt your fishing.

RECOMMENDED FLIES

- Between May and August, an Elk Hair Caddis size 12-16 is always an effective fly for evening fishing.

- Other effective flies include small midges (size 18-24), and bead-headed nymphs.

Nate Lowe '96—Climbing in New Hampshire.

ROCK CLIMBING

C limbing moves outdoor recreation to the vertical plane where an array of technical skills must be learned for safe travel. Students interested in starting to climb should enroll in WOC classes or visit the Nate Lowe Memorial Climbing Wall in the Towne Field House. If you already have experience on the rock, you will find that climbing in the North Berkshire area is limited to small crags that are rarely or poorly described because of unresolved access issues. Williams students should contact the Outing Club for information on Williamstown and other Berkshhire County crags. The purpose of this section is to point you to more distant areas and resources to explore them on your own.

Within a one and a half-hour radius are several larger crags for both top-roping and lead climbing. As access to these areas may change over time, please respect postings and property owners in the area.

ROSE LEDGES

Location: Northfield Farms, MA.
Driving time: 1 hour 20 minutes.
Other info: Top-roping and lead climbing. 40+ routes, many new route possibilities.

HOW TO GET THERE
- Drive east on Route 2 past I-91.
- Turn north on Route 63 and drive approximately 2 mi. to the Northeast Utilities Recreation Area parking lot.

DESCRIPTION
The Rose Ledge Trail takes you to the base of the cliff in about 15 minutes. No formal guidebooks or descriptions are currently avail-

able, both the UMASS Amherst and Hampshire Outing Clubs are good resources for local information on these gneiss cliffs.

CHAPEL LEDGES

Location: Ashfield, MA.
Driving time: 50 minutes.
Other info: Top-roping and lead climbing. 20+ routes, well maintained. Heed notices regarding bird-nesting areas.

HOW TO GET THERE
- Drive east on Route 2 to Route 8 south to Adams.
- Follow signs for Route 116 east. Route 116 will "T" into Route 116/112.
- Take a left, go 2 mi. to Ashfield, follow Route 116 right and go through town.
- 1.6 mi. past Ashfield, 116 bears sharply to the left. Go straight onto a road marked "Williamsburg 9 miles".
- 2.3 mi. along this road is a parking area on the right.

DESCRIPTION
A trail leads to the cliffs from the right side of the road. Across the pavement a dirt road leads to a path to a nice swimming hole. The main attraction of this swimming hole is a 15 foot high natural water slide. Ask local climbers or the Williams Outing Club for more information.

NEW ENGLAND CLIMBING

Due to the lack of very large cliffs in the immediate vicinity, Williams climbers often range much further afield. Most of the best climbing in the Northeastern United States is 2-4 hours from Williams.

The Shawanagunks of southern New York State are perhaps the best known cliffs in the northeast. These beautiful quartz-pebble conglomerate cliffs demand climbing horizontal cracks and pulling through overhangs on big jugs. The "Gunks" are about a two and a half-hour drive southwest of Williamstown. Several guides exist for this area including *The Gunks Guide* by Todd Swain.

Also of note are the basalt cliffs of central Connecticut. Ragged Mountain is a very popular area a little over two hours away. *Hooked on Traprock*, by Ken Nichols, is the most extensive guide, although a short guide specific to Ragged Mountain is also available at most stores in the area.

The White Mountains of New Hampshire provide many fantastic granite cliffs from epic-creating Cannon Mountain to the popular Cathedral and Whitehorse ledges. Information on the White Mountains abounds; Ed Webster's *Rock Climbs in the White Mountains of New Hampshire* is a classic volume.

In upstate New York the Adirondacks are filled with good climbing, including some of the most remote and highest cliffs in the northeast. Towering cliffs of finger ripping anorthosite (an igneous rock) and other metamorphic rocks fill the area. *Climbing in the Adirondacks*, by Don Mellor, provides a detailed guide to both rock and ice climbing in this area.

NATE LOWE MEMORIAL CLIMBING WALL

In 1995 the Williams Outing Club dedicated a 2,000 square-foot climbing wall in memory of Nate Lowe '96, an avid outdoorsman responsible for designing the wall. Since then hundreds of people in the Williams College community have used the artificial wall to learn the basics of climbing safety and technique from experienced and trained student instructor-monitors.

Starting in 1998, 20 semester-long Williamstown community memberships have been offered in the spring and fall for a small fee. Membership allows full access to the climbing wall for the duration of the semester. Climbing wall hours are advertised, but the Williams Outing Club reserves the right to change or eliminate hours without prior notice. If the wall is crowded, preference is given to students, faculty, and staff of Williams College over community members. Community members are not allowed to bring guests to the climbing wall.

PADDLING

The Berkshires offer many scenic and adventure-filled waterways, including several natural lakes and two major rivers. Except for the nearby Hoosic River and Windsor Lake, most areas are a thirty-minute to one-hour drive from Williamstown.

Paddling is most easily enjoyed from early May to October. A favorite time of year is late September when trees cloaked in their autumn color line the banks, and high overhead geese squawk their farewells as they V southward.

Lakes tend to freeze up in January and thaw by early April. However, during this cold period extreme canoeing and whitewater paddling can still be found on some local river sections.

For enjoyable and safe boating, preparation and precaution are essential. Plan your route, including ground transportation, in advance. Dress for the weather, but be prepared for changes – carry extra clothing in a watertight bag. Bring a filled water bottle, quick energy foods, and sun block if necessary. An extra paddle can be helpful, and always travel with others if paddling on whitewater.

For more information, use the references in the bibliography of this book or contact the Outing Club.

EQUIPMENT

As canoeing and kayaking have grown in popularity over the last ten years, so has the difficulty in choosing a boat that best suits your needs among the great variety of models available. Call your local canoe/kayak supplier and find out when they have "demo" days. Test a variety of boat types until you find one that feels comfortable for your skill level. Talk to other boaters to hear their opinions on different designs. Experiment with paddles too, giving attention to length, weight, durability and expense.

When choosing a life vest, a proper fit is most important. It should fit snugly around the torso so that it cannot be easily pulled over one's head. A life vest should also have Coast Guard ratings pertaining to body weight and intended use. It is highly recommended that vests be worn whenever paddling. It is a Massachusetts State law that vests be worn from September 1 – May 1.

Dry bags are rubberized, sealed closure bags that can be filled with extra clothing, food, first aid kit, cameras, and other personal items that need safeguarding from wetness. They should be connected to a canoe thwart to avoid loss during flips, or stuffed snugly inside a kayak's stern compartment. Dry bags can be purchased in stores that outfit water sports.

A throw bag can be very useful if one has experience using it. It is thrown to swimmers in trouble, especially in whitewater situations. At NO time should there be any loose ropes in a canoe or kayak as someone could possibly be entangled and entrapped by them in a flipped boat scenario. Learn how to use a throw rope, as a loose line in the water can be extremely dangerous.

Aqua socks, strap-on rubber sandals, old sneakers or specialty water shoes are good for launching and getting out of boats. If you have wet shoes you are more willing to enter the water and avoid contorted and often dangerous attempts to keep your feet dry. They also provide protection and better footing on rugged rock-strewn river bottoms.

You will need a map and guidebook for put-in and take-out information. They often describe hazards such as dams, quick drops, whitewater and water fluctuations. Guides also generally give distance and time for sections paddled and sometimes include interesting natural history.

To transport a canoe or kayak you need a roof rack for your vehicle. Before setting out, make sure the boat(s) are safely secured to the transport vehicle. The bow, stern, and middle hull should all be tied down to prevent any movement while traveling.

Whitewater enthusiasts need specialized gear and training. For more information we recommend that you find books solely focused on this particular activity. Contact the Williams Outing Club or your local outfitter for specific information and class offerings.

LAKES AND PONDS

Lakes and ponds throughout Berkshire County and surrounding areas are great for leisurely canoe trips or practicing kayak skills for whitewater runs.

WINDSOR LAKE

Location: North Adams.
Driving time: 15 minutes.
Map location: R – 16.

HOW TO GET THERE
- From the junction of Routes 2 and 7, follow Route 2 east.
- At 5.3 mi. the road splits, stay right and descend towards North Adams' town center and Main Street.
- Follow Main St. through a stop light across Route 8a and turn right at a rotary onto Church St at 5.7 miles.
- Drive past Massachusetts College of the Liberal Arts.
- Take your next left onto Bradley Street at 6.4 mi. and ascend a steep hill to Historic Valley Park.

DESCRIPTION
Windsor Lake is a small quiet body of water next to Historic Valley Park, an excellent place for beginner paddlers to learn and practice strokes. There is a beach for public swimming and a playground at the park for young children.

PONTOOSUC LAKE

Location: Pittsfield.
Driving time: 30 minutes.
USGS maps: Pittsfield East, MA & Pittsfield West, MA.

HOW TO GET THERE
- From the junction of Routes 2 and 7, take Route 7 south.

- After driving along Pontoosuc Lake, turn right at a signal light onto Hancock Rd at 17.2 mi.
- Cross over the dam, in a short distance there will be an entrance on the right to public parking and a boat launch.

DESCRIPTION

This is a popular lake for motorboats and jet skis during the summer months. The fishing is good, and there is a swimming beach near the public entrance. Paddling is best during the dawn and dusk light, when the water is calm and quiet, and the sun is low, giving off radiant colors that play on the water.

ONOTA LAKE

Location: Pittsfield.
Driving time: 35 minutes.
USGS map: Pittsfield West, MA.

HOW TO GET THERE

- From the junction of Routes 2 and 7, take Route 7 south towards Pittsfield.
- After driving along Pontoosuc Lake, turn right at a signal light onto Hancock Rd. at 17.2 miles.
- Follow Hancock Rd . and turn left onto Highland Ave. at 18.1 miles.
- Take Highland Ave. to its end. Go straight through signal light (when green!), Highland Ave. becomes Valentine Road.
- There will be a sign for Burbank Park, the public boat access and swimming area for Onota Lake at 19.8 miles.

DESCRIPTION

The **Taconic Range** forms a beautiful backdrop to the west of this large lake. Onota Lake is a great place to see a variety of waterfowl although it does tend to be busy with motorboats during the summer months. This is the home of the Williams College Crew team that has a boathouse on the northeast shore. Regattas take place in the fall and spring. For more information concerning these exciting races, please contact the Williams College Athletic Department.

GRAFTON LAKES

Location: Grafton, NY.
Driving time: 40 minutes.
USGS map: Grafton, NY.

HOW TO GET THERE
- From the junction of Routes 2 and 7, follow Route 7 south.
- At 2.3 mi. turn right onto Route 2 (west) towards Troy, NY.
- Follow Route 2 to the town of Grafton, NY. Look for signs directing you to Grafton Lakes State Park at 15.8 miles.
- Enter the park and follow signs to designated boat launch area.

DESCRIPTION
Long Pond, one of four lakes in Grafton Park, is a favorite for canoeing or kayaking. It is a small body of water with big charm. Birches, beeches, and maples line the shore. Great blue herons stand like statues "wading" patiently for a meal to swim by, and Osprey fly silently above on spiraling currents of wind. This is a great paddle, especially in the fall when the water reflects a myriad of colors from the deciduous trees.

LAUREL LAKE

Distance: Lenox and Lee.
Driving time: 45 minutes.
USGS map: Stockbridge, MA.

HOW TO GET THERE
- From the junction of Routes 2 and 7, take Route 7 south towards Pittsfield.
- Continue through Pittsfield on Route 7 south towards the town of Lee and the Mass Turnpike, follow signs to Route 20 east.
- Take Route 20 east past the Route 7 south intersection.
- Laurel Lake will be on the right side of the road. There is a large paved parking area with a boat launch at 28.5 miles.

DESCRIPTION

Laurel Lake is a great fishing and canoeing spot. There are also two beaches for swimming, one on the east shore, another on the south shore. The lake has some very deep spots where large lake trout and land-locked salmon like to hang out.

STOCKBRIDGE BOWL

Location: Stockbridge.
Driving time: 50 minutes.
USGS map: Stockbridge, MA.

HOW TO GET THERE

- From the junction of Routes 2 and 7, take Route 7 south towards Pittsfield and follow signs to Route 7A Lenox Center.
- Travel through town center, at Lenox monument turn right onto Route 183 south at 26.4 miles.
- Pass the famous Tanglewood music center on the left, stay on Route 183 south.
- A short distance past Tanglewood, is Berkshire Country Day school, on the right side. Immediately after is a large public parking area and boat access on the left side at 28.8 miles. As there is no sign, be careful not to miss the entrance.

DESCRIPTION

The bowl is another fine fishing, canoeing and swimming spot, a great place to boat with a picnic and listen to the wonderful sounds of a Tanglewood concert on a summer day or moonlit evening!

GOOSE POND

Location: Lee.
Driving time: 1 hour.
USGS map: East Lee, MA.

HOW TO GET THERE

- From the junction of Routes 2 and 7, take Route 7 south towards Pittsfield.
- Continue through Pittsfield on Route 7 south towards the town of Lee and the Mass Turnpike, follow signs to Route 20 east.
- Take Route 20 east past the turnoff to the Turnpike, turn right onto Forest St. at 31.6 miles.
- Follow Forest St. until you come to a large grouping of mailboxes on the left side of the road and a state public fishing access sign directing you up a dirt road at 33.7 miles.
- At the top of a hill you will see the boat launch to your right. Please be respectful of the private property postings and park your vehicle along the posted fence.

DESCRIPTION

Goose Pond is a Berkshire jewel located in Lee, Massachusetts. It is made up of lower and upper sections. The lower section is surrounded by private land with many homes along the shore and tends to get busy with small powerboats. Paddle 1.5 mi. east to the upper section and you feel like you are in the middle of a true wilderness area. There is good fishing and great swimming to be found here.

The **Appalachian Trail** is nearby and a wonderful Appalachian Mountain Club cabin maintained for people travelling along the trail is located on the north shore shortly after entering the Upper Goose. Great blue herons, hawks, and beavers are just a few of the frequent visitors to this scenic spot.

Be cautious of the weather, afternoon westerly winds can make paddling quite difficult on the lower section when returning to the boat launch.

SOMERSET RESERVOIR

Location: Somerset, VT.
Driving time: 1.5 hour.
USGS map: Mount Snow, VT & Stratton Mountain, VT.

HOW TO GET THERE

- From the junction of Routes 2 and 7, follow Route 7 north to Bennington.
- In Bennington take Route 9 east (right) at 13.0 miles.
- Follow Route 9 past the junction with Route 8 at 26.5 miles.
- 1.5 mi. beyond the junction look for a sign directing you to Somerset Reservoir and turn left onto Forest Road #71 at 28.0 miles.
- Forest Road quickly becomes a passable gravel/dirt road for the next 9 miles and leads you directly to a public access on the south shore.

DESCRIPTION

This is truly a spectacular place for paddling. Nestled in a remote area surrounded by the Green Mountain National Forest, there is plenty of lake to canoe and kayak. Swimming and fishing are also plentiful. A great overnight trip is to paddle the lake north to Grout Pond where you will find designated camping spots. There is a one mile portage between these two bodies of water. Be cautious of the weather, winds can pick up to quickly churn the water into white caps. Bear, moose and eagles are some of the wildlife that may be seen in this area.

RIVERS

The Berkshire Hills are the headwaters of two beautifu meandering rivers, the Housatonic and the Hoosic. Both are of great recreational value, and provide habitat for numerous species of wildlife. On the eastern boundary of Berkshire Country the Deerfield River flows south and east toward the Connecticut River. For whitewater paddling, sections of the Deerfield offer the best and most challenging rapids.

HOOSIC RIVER

Location: Williamstown & Pownal, VT.
Distance: 5 to 20 minutes.
USGS map: North Adams, MA & Pownal, VT.

HOW TO GET THERE

Following are directions to three boat launch areas in Williamstown and one suggested take-out in Pownal, VT. The descriptions begin with the furthest upstream put-in and continue downstream. Paddlers can certainly choose to put in at any of these launch sites and take out at the next closest one. There is enough current and class 2 rapids to make paddling upstream difficult, so plan on doing a shuttle between put-in and take-out.

Ashton Avenue
- From the junction of Routes 2 and 7, drive east on Route 2 towards North Adams.
- At 2.3 mi. turn left onto Ashton Ave.
- Follow Ashton Ave. 0.2 mi. to a parking area located on the right.

Cole Field (Williams College athletic fields)
- Drive east on Route 2 from Field Park and turn left onto Park St. at 0.2 miles.
- Follow Park and turn right onto Lynde Lane at 0.5 miles.

- Follow Lynde a short distance and then turn left (north) onto Stetson Road at the tennis courts.
- Follow Stetson to Eph's pond and the playing fields.
- At 1.0 mile park to the left, along the barrier. Please do not block the gate or roadway.
- Follow the paved path north towards the river, past a small building to a signed gap in the bushes.

Waste Transfer Station

- From the junction of Routes 2 and 7, take Route 7 north towards Pownal, Vt.
- At 1.2 mi. turn left onto Simonds Road.
- Follow Simonds Rd. over a set of railroad tracks. Immediately past the road to the transfer station there will be a large parking area on the right at 1.4 miles. The put-in is directly across the parking area at the riverbank.

Pownal, Vermont

- From the junction of Routes 2 and 7, follow Route 7 north towards Pownal, Vt.
- At 4.1 mi. turn left onto Route 346 north.
- Follow Route 346 for 0.5 mi. and turn left onto Main St. at 4.6 miles.
- Follow Main St. and turn right onto Lincoln St. (there may not be a sign) – it is the last road on the right before crossing the river.
- Follow Lincoln St. a short distance to a gravel turn out and picnic area on the left at 4.9 miles. You can park here or on the shoulder of Lincoln Street.

DESCRIPTION

From its marshy beginning in Cheshire, Massachusetts, the Hoosic River flows northwestward through Vermont and into New York State where it joins the Hudson River. It offers abundant wildlife, and excellent fishing – though pollutants have rendered the fish inedible. Its meandering course makes for a wonderful paddle. The sections of the Hoosic this guide covers consist of flatwater with a few Class I and Class II whitewater stretches. To avoid low water levels, spring, early summer, and after heavy rains are the best times to paddle. There may be water hazards such as tree blowdowns that you should be watchful for.

From the Ashton Avenue put-in the approximate paddling distances are: 2.4 mi. to Cole Field, 3.9 mi. to the Waste Transfer Station, and 8.9 mi. to the Pownal take-out.

HOUSATONIC RIVER

Location: Lenox and Lenoxdale.
Driving time: 45 minutes.
USGS map: Pittsfield East, MA and East Lee, MA.

There are several great paddling sections of the Housatonic River. The following is a favorite of the Williams Outing Club.

HOW TO GET THERE
- From the junction of Routes 2 and 7, take Route 7 south through Pittsfield.
- Turn left onto New Lenox Road at 23.5 miles.
- Follow through an intersection and over railroad tracks; just before crossing over the river, there will be a sign directing you into the John F. Decker boat launch on the right side of the road at 24.9 miles.
- Due to limited parking, please park in the adjacent lot to the west once you unload boats and gear.

DESCRIPTION
The Housatonic River begins in the Berkshire Hills and winds its way 150 miles south where it empties into Long Island Sound. There are several excellent paddling forays that range from gentle meandering currents to exciting whitewater.

The section described here is a very enjoyable paddle past farmlands, and through protected state Fisheries and Wildlife land. It is a great place to watch for wildlife, especially birds during the migratory and nesting seasons. The looming October Mountain in the east presents a spectacular wall of color in the fall.

From the Decker launch, the river twists and turns gently for approximately 6 miles until it reaches Woods Pond. The current is almost negligible, although you can see aquatic plant life pointing downstream. It is very possible to paddle down and return upstream, or you can shuttle a car to the *Woods Pond take out.

The Housatonic is boatable all year long except in a deep, deep freeze. This is a highly recommended trip, especially for beginners.

For more historical information and details about other paddleable sections refer to *A Canoeing Guide for the Housatonic River in Berkshire County.*

*Woods Pond Take Out from Decker Launch

- Turn left onto New Lenox Rd., cross over railroad tracks and turn left at the stop sign onto East St. at 0.6 miles.
- Follow East St. to an intersection with Housatonic St. and turn left at 3.4 miles.
- Follow Housatonic St. to the end, turn left onto Willow Creek Rd. at 4.3 miles. There will be a large parking area in front of the old Lenox train station. The station has been converted into a wonderful model train museum. It is now called the Berkshire Scenic Railway Museum. Definitely worth a visit after a nice paddle.

DEERFIELD RIVER

Location: Fife Brook – Florida, Massachusetts
Driving time: 35 minutes
USGS map: North Adams, MA & Rowe, MA

There are several exciting sections of this river that range from Class I to Class V whitewater. The Fife Brook stretch has Class II and III rapids and is a popular section for WOC kayak instruction.

HOW TO GET THERE
- From the junction of Routes 2 and 7, take Route 2 East towards North Adams.
- Follow Route 2 past North Adams up and over the famous "hairpin." Turn at first left after the bronzed elk historical marker onto Whitcomb Hill Road at 12.6 miles.

- Follow the steep winding Whitcomb Hill Road all the way to the end, turn left onto River Road heading towards Monroe.
- Follow River Road for 2 mi., bear right onto a road directing you to a catch-and-release fishing area. Park along the shoulder or at designated parking near out houses. Look for trails leading a short walk to the put-in.
- If shuttling with a vehicle, follow River Road downstream 4.9 miles. Immediately after the Zoar Gap bridge is a parking area on the right. This is a good place to check out the class III rapids of Zoar Gap.

DESCRIPTION

From its beginnings in the Green Mountains of Vermont, this once wild river, now tamed by a series of dams, runs southeastward until it meets up with the Connecticut River. Newly developed river flow policies have been established to create a more consistent release calendar that benefits fishermen and boaters. This has caused a surge in the river's recreational popularity. The Deerfield is considered one of the best whitewater runs in the northeast when the dams let loose.

Two sections in particular are best for whitewater excitement.. The Fife Brook run is made up of mainly class I and II rapids. However, there is a challenging class III stretch of water through the Zoar Gap approximately five miles downstream from the put in. If paddling this for the first time, scout the gap before entering.

There is a pull-out on river left, across from an obvious prominent steep highway department created embankment. You can walk up to the nearby railroad tracks and follow them downstream until you reach a path leading to a view of the gap. Be mindful that the tracks are still in use and that you are walking on private property.

The second section, known as the Monroe Bridge Dryway, is extremely popular among experienced kayakers, canoeists and rafters. It is classified as a Class III and IV run. It is just north of the Fife Brook dam. For more detailed information about this section and others on the Deerfield River refer to *The Deerfield River Guidebook*.

BIBLIOGRAPHY

STARTING OUT & OUTDOOR TRAVEL

Drury, Jack K. and Bruce F. Bonney. *The Backcountry Classroom*. Merrillville, IN. ICS Books Inc., 1992.

Kjellstrom, Bjorn. *Be Expert with Map and Compass*. Macmillar General Reference, 1994.

Hampton, Bruce and David Cole. *Soft Paths: How to Enjoy the Wilderness Without Harming It*, rev. Stackpole Books, 1995.

McGiveny, Annette. *Leave No Trace: A Practical Guide to the New Wilderness Ethic*. Seattle, WA. Mountaineers Books, 1998.

Meyer, Kathleen. *How to Shit in the Woods*. Berkeley, CA. Ten Speed Press, 1989.

Petzoldt, Paul and Raye Carleson Ringholz. *The New Wilderness Handbook*. New York. W.W. Norton & Company, 1984.

Randall, Glen. *The Outward Bound Map and Compass Handbook*. New York. Lyons and Burford, 1989.

Richard, Sukey, Donna Orr, and Claudia Lindholm. *NOLS Cookery*, 3rd ed. Mechanicsburg, PA. Stackpole Books, 1991.

FIRST AID

Isaac, Jeff and Peter Goth. *The Outward Bound Wilderness First Aid Handbook*. New York. Lyons and Burford, 1991.

Schimelpfenig, Todd and Linda Lindsey. *NOLS Wilderness First Aid*. Mechanicsburg, PA. Stackpole Books, 1991.

Tilton, Buck and Frank Hubbell. *Medicine for the Backcountry*. Indiana. ICS Books Inc., 1990.

Wilkerson, James A. *Medicine for Mountaineering*. Seattle, WA. Mountaineers Books, 1982.

HISTORY

Brooks, Robert R.R., ed. *Williamstown: The First 200 Years 1753-1953*. Williamstown Historical Commission, 1974.

Burns, Deborah E. and Lauren R. Stevens. *Most Excellent Majesty: A History of Mount Greylock*. Pittsfield, MA. Berkshire Natural Resources Council, 1988.

Carney, William. *A Berkshire Sourcebook*. Pittsfield, MA. Junior League of Berkshire County, 1976.

Giller, Jeremy. "A Brief History of the Williams Outing Club," Williamstown, MA. 1993.

Livingston, Mark "A Portraiture of Stone Hill: Lying Between Green River and Hemlock Brook in Williamstown." Williamstown, MA. Williams College Center for Environmental Studies, 1972.

Perry, Arthur L. *Origins in Williamstown*. 1894.

Williams Outing Club, "The Blaze," Spring 1956.

"The 1931-1932 Season of the Williams Outing Club" (anon., yearbook memorandum).

Williams Outing Club Archives.

NATURAL HISTORY

Hendricks, Bartlett. *Birds of Berkshire County*. Pittsfield, MA. The Berkshire Museum, 1994.

Kricher, John. *A Field Guide to Eastern Forests*. Boston, MA. Houghton Mifflin, 1988.

Laubach, René. *A Guide to Natural Places in the Berkshire Hills*. Stockbridge, MA. Berkshire House Publishers, 1992.

Marchand, Peter. *North Woods: An Inside Look at the Nature of Forests in the Northeast*. Boston, MA. Appalachian Mountain Club Books, 1987.

Newcomb, Lawrence. *Newcomb's Wildflower Guide*. Boston, MA. Little, Brown and Company, 1977.

Strauch, Joseph, G., Jr. *Wildflowers of the Berkshires and Taconic Hills*. Stockbridge, MA. Berkshire House Publishers, 1995.

Weatherbee, Pamela. *Flora of Berkshire County Massachusetts*. The Berkshire Museum, 1996.

Williams Naturalists. *Farms to Forest: A Naturalist's Guide to the Ecology and Human History of Hopkins Memorial Forest*. Williamstown, MA. Center for Environmental Studies, 1995.

GUIDES TO TRAILS IN BERKSHIRE COUNTY

Appalachian Mountain Club. *AMC Massachusetts and Rhode Island Trail Guide*, 6th ed. Boston, MA. Appalachian Mountain Club Books, 1989.

League of Woman Voters. *Runner's Guide to Williamstown*. Williamstown, MA.

Ryan, Christopher J. *Guide to the Taconic Trail System*. Amherst, MA. New England Cartographics, 1989.

Smith, Charles W.G. *Nature Walks in the Berkshire Hills*. Boston, MA. Appalachian Mountain Club Books, 1997.

Stevens, Lauren R. *Hikes and Walks in the Berkshire Hills*.rev. Stockbridge, MA. Berkshire House Publishers, 1998.

Taconic Hiking Club. *Guide to the Taconic Crest Trail*. Troy, NY. Taconic Hiking Club, 1988.

Williams Outing Club.*WOC Trail Guide and Map*, 8th ed. Williamstown, MA. Williams Outing Club, 1988.

Williams Trail Commission. *The Mountains of Eph: A Guidebook of the Williams Outing Club*. Williamstown, MA. Williams Outing Club, 1927.

GUIDES TO TRAILS IN NEW ENGLAND

Appalachian Mountain Club. *AMC White Mountain Guide*, 26th ed. Boston, MA. Appalachian Mountain Club Books, 1998.

Appalachian Trail Conference. *Appalachian Trail Guide to Massachusetts and Connecticut with Northern Berkshire Trails*, 9th ed. Harper's Ferry, WV. 1994.

Brady, John and Brian White. *Fifty Hikes in Massachusetts*. Woodstock, VT. Backcountry Publications, 1983.

Dartmouth Outing Club. *The Dartmouth Outing Guide*. Hanover, NH. 1992.

Goodwin, Tony, ed. *Guide to Adirondack Trails: High Peaks Region*, 12th ed. Series. Adirondack Mountain Club. 1992.

Green Mountain Club. *Guide Book of the Long Trail*, 23rd ed. Waterbury Center, VT. 1992.

Green Mountain Club. *Day Hiker's Guide to Vermont*, 3rd ed. Waterbury Center, VT. 1990.

Mikolas, Mark. *Nature Walks in Southern Vermont*. Boston, MA. Appalachian Mountain Club, 1995.

Perry, John and Jane Greverus Perry. *The Sierra Club Guide to the Natural Areas of New England*. San Fransisco, CA. Sierra Club Books, 1990.

WINTER

Fredston, Jill A. and Doug Fesler. *Snow Sense*. Anchorage AK. Alaska Mountain Safety Center, Inc., 1994.

Goodman, David. *Classic Backcountry Skiing*. Boston, MA. Appalachian Mountain Club Books, 1989.

Gorman, Stephen. *AMC Guide to Winter Camping*.

O'Bannon, Allen and Mike Clelland. *Allen and Mike's Really Cool Backcountry Ski Book*. Evergreen, CO. Chockstone Press, 1996.

Parker, Paul. *Free-Heel Skiing*, 2nd ed. Seattle, WA. Mountaineers Books, 1995.

Stevens, Lauren R. *Skiing in the Berkshire Hills*. Stockbridge, MA. Berkshire House Publishers, 1991.

BIKING

Bridge, Raymond. *Bike Touring: The Sierra Club's Guide to Outings on Wheels*. San Francisco, CA. Sierra Club Books, 1987.

Cuyler, Lewis C. *Bike Rides in the Berkshire Hills*. Stockbridge, MA. Berkshire House Publishers, 1991.

Duling, Sandy. *Short Bike Rides, Vermont*. Old Saybrook, CT. The Globe Pequot Press, 1997.

Immler, Robert M. *The Mountain Biker's Guide to Ski Resorts*. Woodstock, VT. Backcountry Publications, 1998.

Williams Outing Club. *WOC Bicycling Guide and Map*. Williamstown, MA. WOC, 1981.

FISHING

Hughes, Dave. *Reading the Water: A Fly Fisher's Handbook for Finding Trout in All Types of Water*. Mechanicsburg, PA. Stackpole Books, 1988.

Hughes, Dave. *Tactics for Trout*. Mechanicsburg, PA. Stackpole Books, 1990.

Lessels, Bruce and Norman Sims. *The Deerfield River Guidebook*. North Amherst, MA. New England Cartographics, 1993. (Fishing section by Jim Dowd).

Meck, Charles R. *Fishing Small Streams With a Fly Rod.* Woodstock, NY. Countryman Press, 1991.

O'Reilly, Pat. *River Trout Fishing: Expert Advice for Beginners (Fishing Facts).* North Pomfret, VT. Trafalgar Square, 1992.

CLIMBING

Graydom, Don and Kurt Hanson, ed. *Mountaineering: The Freedom of the Hills*, 6th ed. Seattle, WA. Mountaineers Books, 1997.

Long, John. *How to Rock Climb,* 3rd ed. Evergreen, CO. Chockstone Press, 1998.

Powers, Phil. *NOLS Wilderness Mountaineering.* Mechanicsburg, PA. Stackpole Books, 1993.

Mellor, Don. *Climbing in the Adirondacks: A Guide to Rock and Ice Routes in the Adirondack Park.* Lake George, NY. Adirondack Mountain Club, 1995.

Nichols, Ken. *Hooked on Traprock: Rock Climbing in Central Connecticut.* Mattituck, NY. Amereon House, 1995.

Swain, Todd. *The Gunks Guide.* Evergreen CO. Chockstone Press, 1995.

Webster, Ed. *Rock Climbs in the White Mountains of New Hampshire.* Eldorado Springs, CO. Mountain Imagery, 1996.

PADDLING

Appalchian Mountain Club. *AMC River Guide: New Hampshire and Vermont.* Boston, MA. Appalachian Mountain Club Books, 1989.

Bechdel, Les and Slim Ray. *River Rescue,* 2nd ed. Boston, MA. Appalachian Mountain Club Books, 1989.

Berkshire County Regional Planning Commission and Housatonic Valley Association. *A Conoeing Guide for the Housatonic River in Berkshire County.*

Borton, Mark C., ed. *The Complete Boating Guide to the Connecticut Rivers.* Woodstock, VT. Backcountry Publications, 1985.

Lessels, Bruce and Norman Sims. *The Deerfield River Guidebook.* North Amherst, MA. New England Cartographics, 1993.

Schweiker, Roiloli, ed. *AMC River Guide: Massachusetts, Connecticut, Rhode Island.* Boston, MA. Appalachian Mountain Club Books, 1985.

RESOURCES

EQUIPMENT AND SUPPLIES

The Mountain Goat
Outdoor clothing, gear and service.
Bicycling, nordic skiing, backpacking and camping.
130 Water Street • Williamstown, MA 01267
(413) 458-8445

The Spoke Bicycles
Bicycle equipment, repair and service.
620 Main Street • Williamstown, MA 01267
(413) 458-3456

Wild Oats Community Market
Non-profit consumers' cooperative food market.
Natural, organic and bulk foods.
Colonial Shopping Center • Williamstown, MA 01267
(413) 458-8060

Berkshire Outfitters
Outdoor equipment, repairs and service.
Paddlesports and nordic skiing.
Route 8 • Adams, MA 01220
(413) 743-5900 • http://berkshireoutfitters.com

The Arcadian Shop
Outdoor clothing, equipment and service.
91 Pittsfield Road • Lenox, MA 01240
(313) 637-3010 • http://www.arcadian.com/

Ski Fanatics
Alpine ski equipment.
20 Williamstown Road • Lanesboro, MA 01237
(413) 443-3023 • http://www.skifanatics.com

BOOKSTORES
Water Street Books
Full service bookstore with outdoor literature.
26 Water Street • Williamstown, MA 01267
(413) 458-8071 • http://www.waterstreet.bookstore.com

The Mountaineers
Member-supported club with active outing, instructional and publishing departments.
300 3rd Ave • W Seattle, WA 98119
(206) 284-6310 • http://www.mountaineers.org

LOCAL ORGANIZATIONS AND GOVERNMENT AGENCIES
Appalachian Mountain Club (regional office)
Manages Bascom Lodge on Mt. Greylock, conducts educational program and publishes information on the area.
Mt. Greylock Visitor Center
P.O. Box 1800 • Lanesboro, MA 01237
(413) 443-0011

Center for Environmental Studies
For information about Hopkins Memorial Forest.
Kellogg House, Williams College • Williamstown, MA 01267
(413) 597-2346 • http://www.williams.edu/CES

Department of Environmental Management
For information about outdoor recreation in Berkshire County.
Berkshire Region Headquarters • Pittsfield, MA 01202
(413) 442-8928 • http://www.magnet.state.ma.us

Massachusetts Division of Fisheries and Wildlife
Conservation of land for protection of wildlife.
400 Hubbard Ave. • Pittsfield, MA 01201
(413)447-9789

Hoosic River Watershed Association
Works to protect, preserve and restore the Hoosic River and surrounding watershed.
P.O. Box 667 • Williamstown, MA 01267
(413) 458-2742

Berkshire Wildlife Sanctuaries
Massachusetts Audubon Society
472 W. Mountain Road • Lenox, MA 01240
(413) 637-0320 • http://www.massaudubon.org

New York Department of Environmental Conservation (DEC)
Division of Lands and Forests
Owns and manages land along the Taconic Crest.
50 Wolf Road • Albany, NY 12233
(518) 457-2475

Taconic Hiking Club
For information about the Taconic Crest Trail.
c/o Wolfe
45 Kakely Street • Albany, NY 12208
(518) 482-0424

Town of Williamstown
Town Hall
31 North St. • Williamstown 01267
(413) 458-9341 • http://www.williamstown.net

The Trustees of Reservations
A private nonprofit member organization dedicated to preserving properties of exceptional scenic, historic, and ecological value.
572 Essex Street • Beverly, MA 01915
(413) 298-3239 • http://www.ttor.org

Williams Outing Club
Williams College student outdoor organization.
1004 Baxter Hall • Williamstown, MA 01267
(413) 597-2317 • http://wso.williams.edu/orgs/woc/

Williamstown Rural Lands Foundation
Non-profit, member-supported Land Trust for the
Williamstown area.
18-B Spring Street • P.O. Box 221• Williamstown, MA 01267
(413) 458-2494 • http://www2.shore.net/~mltc

OTHER ORGANIZATIONS

Adirondack Mountain Club
A non-profit membership organization dedicated to conservation,
recreation and education in the Adirondack Mountains. Maintains
trails, lean-tos, huts and lodges. Publishes books and maps.
814 Goggins Road • Lake George, NY 12845
(800)395-8080 • http://www.global2000.net/ADK/home.html

Appalachian Mountain Club
A non-profit membership organization. Maintains huts, lodges and
trails throughout the northeast for public use. Publishes books
and maps for outdoor adventures in the eastern U.S.
5 Joy Street • Boston, MA 02108
(617)523-0636 • http://wwwoutdoors.org

Appalachian Trail Conference
Coordinating body for Appalachian Trail management. Publishes
a series of ten guidebooks for the trail.
P.O. Box 807 • Harper's Ferry, WV 25425
(304) 535-6331 • http://www.atconf.org

Green Mountain Club
A membership organization that maintains and protects the Long
Trail and other hiking byways in Vermont.
4711 Waterbury-Stowe Rd. • Waterbury Center, VT 05677
(802)244-7037 • http://www.greenmountainclub.org

National Outdoor Leadership School (NOLS)
A wilderness-based, non-profit school focusing on leadership and
skills. NOLS has four branches in the U.S. as well as one each in
Canada, Mexico, Kenya and Chile.
288 Main St. • Lander, WY 82520-3140
(307)332-6973 • http://www.nols.edu

Outward Bound USA
Wilderness courses designed to inspire self-esteem, self-reliance, concern for others and care for the environment. Outward Bound has five schools in the United States.
100 Mystery Point Rd. • Garrison, NY 10524
888-882-6863 • http://www.outwardbound.com

SOLO Wilderness Medicine
Offers courses in Wilderness Medicine from First Aid to WEMT.
P.O Box 3150
Conway, NH 03818
(603) 447-6711 • http://www.stonehearth.com

Distribution Branch
To order U.S. Geological Survey Maps.
U. S. Geological Survey
Box 25286, Federal Center, Bldg. 41 • Denver, CO 80225
http://www.nmd.usgs.gov

Wilderness Medical Associates
189 Dudley Rd • Bryant Pond, ME 04219
(888)WILD-MED (888) 945-3633 • http://www.wildmed.com

Wilderness Medicine Institute
Providing quality education for the recognition, treatment and prevention of wilderness emergencies.
P.O. Box 9 • 413 Main St. • Pitkin, CO 81241
(970)641-3572 • http://www.wildernessmed.com

INDEX